ex Libris

McMurtry

THE LIGHT OF OTHER DAYS

The light of other days

A selection of monuments, mausoleums and memorials in Church of Ireland churches and graveyards and those whom they commemorate

Sam Hutchison

Wordwell

First published in 2008
Wordwell Ltd
Media House, South County Business Park
Leopardstown, Dublin 18, Ireland
Copyright © The author

Cover design: Nick Maxwell and Rachel Dunne

ISBN 978 1 905569 19 9

British Library Cataloguing-in-Publication Data.
A catalogue record for this book is available from the British Library.

This publication has received support from the Heritage Council under the 2003 Publications Grant Scheme.

Typeset in Ireland by Wordwell Ltd.

Editor: Emer Condit.

Book design: Nick Maxwell.

All photographs by the author unless otherwise stated.

Printed by Castuera, Pamplona.

Contents

Foreword

Sam Hutchison has travelled extensively in Ireland to gather the information contained in this fascinating book. His photographs make identification easy and are an encouragement to have a copy readily available no matter where one might travel in Ireland. This is not a comprehensive catalogue but rather a personal collection that provides an introduction to the variety of monuments and memorials to be found in Church of Ireland churches. They reflect various times and social styles. Many are simple and others are pretentious. Some show very fine sculpture and dramatic emotion, and many are illustrative of the life and work of the individuals commemorated. Soldiers, seamen, architects, musicians, writers and clergy are all represented.

This collection should alert us to the potential loss of important monuments where churches are under threat of closure. The stories that lie behind the monuments can be particularly poignant and remind us of earlier times in Ireland.

I'm sure you will be as intrigued as I was when you read these pages.

Desmond Harman[†]
Dean of Christ Church Cathedral (2004–2007)

Preface

When I read the several dates of the tombs, of some that died yesterday, and some six hundred years ago, I consider that great day when we shall all of us be contemporaries, and make our appearance together.

Joseph Addison
(1672–1719)

There are thousands of memorials in Church of Ireland cathedrals and churches; St Patrick's Cathedral holds more than 200, while many churches have up to 50 and sometimes more, as at St Mary's, Athlone, Co. Westmeath. There are also churches that are themselves memorials: a beautiful example is the Adelaide Memorial Church of Christ the Redeemer, Myshall, Co. Carlow, built by John Duguid Dover in memory of his daughter Constance. Headstones in church graveyards are numbered in tens of thousands.

The aim of this book is twofold: firstly to describe a representative selection, and secondly to tell something of the lives of those they commemorate. By doing so I hope to draw attention to aspects of Irish history that are little known by the general public, and to encourage people to seek out memorials in their own neighbourhood. There are few churches that do not have some story to tell. Memorials, by their very nature, make us pause and reflect on the great mysteries of life and death. Many in Ireland have a particular poignancy as they remember families, once powerful and influential, who left the country never to return. Like those tablets to Roman centurions in the museums near Hadrian's Wall, they remind us of an alien people who came, saw, conquered, did much good as well as harm, and finally left.

Sadly, the stock of memorials and monuments open to the public gaze is dwindling all the time. As churches are deconsecrated—and this was the fate of hundreds in the twentieth century—their contents are put in peril. When a church is boarded up, the monuments are frequently imprisoned within. When the building is required for another use, it is often gutted and its artefacts dispersed. When the fine old church of St Mary in Kilkenny city was closed and put to another use, all of its many interesting and artistic memorials were transferred to what was once the north transept and locked away. Only by the expenditure of a great deal of money (not usually available) and the finding of a suitable home will these historical items ever be available for viewing by the public again. Another problem is wear and tear, with so many going back to the eighteenth century. Christ Church Cathedral is in the process of restoring some of its finest monuments but it is a very expensive and painstaking business.

My research for this book covered a period of over three years, during which I visited several hundred churches in all 32 counties. Except on Sunday, access to the vast majority required an appointment and someone to open the door, and I am most grateful to all those who so willingly helped me, some of whom had to travel considerable distances. Many gave me valuable information and were helpful in other ways. I also have to acknowledge my debt to Homan Potterton, whose book *Irish church monuments 1570–1880* was invaluable in tracing material of which otherwise I would have been unaware. My thanks are also due to my cousin Graham Watchorn, a professional surveyor of churches and their contents, for his help and guidance. Finally and lovingly I give most grateful thanks to my daughter, Linda, for typing my scribbles so willingly and well. She did most of this work in 2005 in between looking after her daughter, Jane, born in January of the same year. Full marks on both counts!

Desmond Harman, Dean of Christchurch Cathedral, Dublin, (2004–7), who kindly contributed the foreword, sadly passed away before the book went to press. Both the publisher and I hope that his family will be glad to see his name associated with a subject that was of great interest to him.

In memory of my mother and father

1. RATHDOWN SLABS

The graveyards of the Church of Ireland are nearly always interesting and peaceful—islands of calm in an increasingly noisy and crowded world. The playwright Samuel Beckett, who was born into a Church of Ireland family, has this to say on the subject: 'Personally, I have no bone to pick in graveyards. I take the air willingly, perhaps more willingly than elsewhere, when the air I must. My sandwich, my banana taste sweeter when I am sitting on a tomb.'

Graveyards also bring to light occasional surprises. The archaeologist Chris Corlett missed his bus in Dundrum, Co. Dublin, one day in 2002, and with time to spare took the opportunity to visit the ancient graveyard of St Nahi's Church. Out of the corner of his eye he spied an incised granite stone sticking out of the ground and, intrigued, decided to return later with a view to having it raised and examined. Unfortunately, by the time he did so the exposed portion had been unwittingly smashed with a sledgehammer. When the main and intact part was raised, however, he was excited to discover what is known as a Rathdown Slab.

Rathdown Slabs feature a distinctive type of decoration but no two are exactly the same. The most common motif is a herringbone design and cupmarks, often enclosed by concentric circles. The slab found at St Nahi's is made from a piece of reddish granite and features a cupmark and a saltire cross. Rathdown Slabs have been found at many old church sites in south-east Dublin and neighbouring parts of Wicklow but not elsewhere in Ireland. Today they are generally regarded as having been influenced by Viking art styles and almost certainly marked the graves of Christians who were probably of Viking descent. All of this suggests that the Vikings played an important role in the development of the churches in the area. Originally the slabs would have lain flat on the ground.

1. Part of a Rathdown Slab at St Nahi's, Dundrum, Co. Dublin.

In 2004 part of a second slab was found in the same graveyard and both are on display in the baptistry of St Nahi's. While it is not possible to date them precisely, it is believed that the Vikings of Dublin had converted to Christianity by the year 980, which suggests that they are at least 1,000 years old. If so, they are probably the most ancient memorials in any Church of Ireland church.

2. THE YEARS 1400 TO 1700

Rathdown Slabs apart, there are few memorials that pre-date 1400. An exception is the tomb and effigy identified as that of Richard FitzGilbert or Strongbow (died 1176) in Christ Church Cathedral and dated *c*. 1330. The original monument to this powerful Norman baron, however, was broken by the fall of the cathedral roof in 1562 and replaced by the present similar monument, probably to Thomas Fitzgerald, eighth earl of Desmond, in 1570. Be that as it may, to Dubliners and the thousands of visitors who come to the cathedral each year the effigy is that of Strongbow and is likely to remain so.

After 1400, one of the earliest and most interesting monuments is the tomb of James Rice, eleven times lord mayor of Waterford, placed in that city's old cathedral in 1481 and now in the Georgian cathedral built on the same site. It is somewhat gruesome but typical of the type of memorial inspired by the Black Death in the fourteenth century, when the bubonic plague reduced the European population by almost 50%. Rice is shown in effigy, his badly decayed body crawling with worms and a frog feeding on his stomach. Part of the inscription reads:

> 'I am what you will be
> I was what you are now'.

Another horrifying monument, dated *c*. 1520, is in the churchyard of St Peter's, Drogheda, Co. Louth. It depicts two decomposing skeletal bodies, and commemorates Sir Edmund Golding and his wife Elizabeth Flemying.

A tomb-chest dated 1482 with recumbent, fully clothed effigies of Lord Portlester (Sir Roland FitzEustace) and his wife Margaret is in the tower of St Audoen's Church, Dublin. Another in memory of Archbishop Michael Tregury (1449–71), with his effigy in relief, is in St Patrick's Cathedral. These decorated tomb-chests, the sides of

3

2. *Detail from a seventeenth-century tomb in Derry Cathedral.*

3. *Detail from the Duff memorial at St Audoen's, Dublin.*

which are often carved with saints, angels, apostles and the like, continued to be popular into the sixteenth century; that of Piers Butler, 8th earl of Ormonde (who died in 1539), and his wife Margaret, in Kilkenny Cathedral, is a good and well-preserved example.

4. The 8th earl of Ormonde and his wife Margaret in Kilkenny Cathedral.

The altar-tomb effigy of Bishop Wellesley, who also died in 1539, is considered to be the finest surviving monument of the period and has been described by Peter Harbison as 'a very noble and well proportioned work, of a quality far above that of all other contemporary sculptures in Anglo-Norman Ireland'. In 1971 it was brought from the ruined priory of Grand Connell to its present resting-place in Kildare Cathedral by the 7th duke of Wellington. Surprisingly, if somewhat discreetly, it incorporates a sheelagh-na-gig amongst a variety of carvings.

As the sixteenth century progressed and the Elizabethan plantations consolidated themselves, family funerals became more lavish and extravagant. Memorials were correspondingly more lifelike. The nobility no longer lay recumbent but raised themselves up and leaned on their elbow or knelt in prayer. They were attended by family members, also on their knees, the whole contained within an architectural framework of classical columns and niches. An early but small-scale example is the alabaster wall memorial in Christ Church Cathedral, Dublin, to Sir Francis Agard, soldier and counsellor, who died in 1577. On the left,

kneeling, are Sir Francis, his wife and three of his children, and on the right his daughter Cecilie and her two children. The memorial was erected in 1584, the year Cecilie died, by her husband, Sir Henry Harrington.

The north wall of St Audoen's Church, Dublin, features two stucco monuments similar in design to that for the Agard family but with more detail and dated to between 1625 and 1640. The one on the left is of the Sparke family, who were Protestant, and that on the right the Duff family, who were Catholic, which reflects the confused loyalties typical of the period. Both monuments would originally have been brightly coloured, and there are plans to restore them to their former state.

The 1634 memorial in Donadea Church, Co. Kildare, to Sir Gerald Aylmer, his wife Julia, his son and daughter is attractive but restrained and suggests a simple piety. The same is true of the small 1619 monument to Sir Richard Hansard and his wife Anne in Clonleigh Parish Church, Lifford, Co. Donegal, which shows them kneeling opposite one another across a draped reading desk.

In complete contrast, the tomb erected by Richard Boyle, 1st earl of Cork (1566–1643), in St Patrick's Cathedral in 1632 is large, ostentatious and divided into four tiers. It contains sixteen figures, representing members of his family—including, it is believed, his

6. *Bishop Wellesley (d. 1539) in Kildare Cathedral.*

7. *Tomb of Richard Boyle, 1st earl of Cork, in St Mary's, Youghal, Co. Cork.*

youngest son, Robert Boyle (1627–91), the famous chemist, whose work on gases and vacuums led to the law that bears his name. The tomb, by Edward Tingham of Dublin, was originally erected in the cathedral choir, but two years later was dismantled and put into boxes by order of the arrogant lord deputy, the earl of Strafford, an enemy of Boyle's. It was only moved to its present position at the west end of the nave in 1863.

Boyle, known as the Great Earl, was one of the richest and most successful of the early Elizabethan planters and owned vast tracts of land. In 1620, prior to the erection of the Dublin monument and perhaps to hedge his bets, he had another memorial raised in St Mary's Church, Youghal, Co. Cork. This is by Alexander Hills of London and is more modest in scale. The earl reclines in the centre, below his family tree, with his first wife, Alice Apsley, to the left and his second, Katherine Fenton, to the right. Those of his fourteen children born by 1619 kneel below, while his mother-in-law, Lady Fenton, who reclines at the top, ensures that all is in order.

The most splendid seventeenth-century tomb anywhere in Ireland was erected in St Nicholas's Parish Church, Carrickfergus, Co. Antrim, to commemorate Sir Arthur Chichester (died 1625) and his wife Lettice (died 1620). They are shown kneeling in prayer with their dead infant between them. Below, also kneeling, is Sir Arthur's brother, Sir John, who was ambushed and beheaded by the MacDonnells in 1597. Homan Potterton describes the tomb, whose sculptor is unknown, as 'the most elaborate and exquisite of its type surviving in Ireland'. Sir Arthur was lord deputy of Ireland from 1605 to 1615 and the principal beneficiary of the Elizabethan land settlement in Ulster; he was also the founder of Belfast.

Another monument of the same type, but defaced and badly damaged by Cromwellian soldiers, is that in St Mary's Cathedral, Limerick, to the earl of Thomond, who died in 1624, and his wife Elizabeth Fitzgerald.

A fine black and white marble wall monument in St Columb's Cathedral, Derry, commemorates two heroes of the great siege of that city in 1689. Colonel Henry Baker, the military governor, died 'worn out by hardship and disease' on the 74th day of the siege, while Captain Michael Browning of the relieving ship *Mountjoy* was killed at the boom in the River Foyle 'in the hour of victory' on 28 July 1689.

Captain James Hamilton was killed at the Battle of Benburb on

8. Outside
Dromore
Cathedral: 'Here
lies the body of
Brian Shorten—
died November,
1680'.

9. Detail from the seventeenth-century monument to Archbishop Jones in St Patrick's Cathedral, Dublin.

HERE ARE INTERRED THE BODY OF
ABRAHAM GILLOTT WHO DIED THE
8th OF JULY 1711 AGED 55 YEARS
ANN WIFE OF SAMUEL LEWIS
CROMMELIN WHO DIED THE 30th
OF AUGUST 1718 AGED 30 YEARS
GILLOTT THEIR SON WHO DIED 2nd
OF DECEMBER 1715 AGED 2 YEARS
JANE THEIR DAUGHTER WHO DIED
THE 31st OF JANUARY 1718 AGED 5
MONTHS. HENRIETTE SECOND
WIFE OF SAMUEL LEWIS CROMM-
ELIN WHO DIED THE 19th OF MAY
1739 AGED 57 YEARS. EASTHER
WIFE OF JAMES CROMMELIN
DIED THE 2nd OF SEPTEMBER 1739
AGED 41 YEARS SAMUEL LEWIS
CROMMELIN WHO DIED THE 2nd
OF SEPTEMBER 1713 AGED 57 YEARS
HIS DAUGHTERS ANN DIED 21st OF
JUNE 1751 AGED 27 YEARS
HENRIETTE 28th OF MARCH 1752
AGED 23 YEARS MAGDALEN 18th
APRIL 1753 AGED 25 YEARS

SIX FOOT OPPOSITE LYES THE
BODY OF LOUIS CROMMELIN
BORN AT ST. QUENTIN FRANCE
ONLY SON TO LOUIS CROMM-
ELIN AND ANN CROMMELIN
DIRECTOR OF THE LINEN MAN-
UFACTORY WHO DIED BELOVED
OF ALL AGED 28 YEARS THE 1st OF
JULY 1711
SISTE VIATOR ET UT ILLE DUM VITA
MANNEBAT SUSPICE COELUM DES-
PICE MUNDUM ET RESPICE FINEM
ALSO THE BODY OF MARY MAD-
ELIENE BERNIERE WIFE OF
CAPTAIN BERNIERE ONLY DAUGH-
TER OF LEWIS CROMMELIN
DECEASED THE 8th OF JULY 1715
AGED 21 YEARS
HERE ALSO LYETH THE REMAINS OF
LOUIS CROMMELIN SENR WHO
DIED 7th JULY 1727 AGED 75 YEARS
ALSO THE BODY OF ANNE WIFE
OF LOUIS CROMMELIN DECEAS-
ED THE 15th AUGUST 1755 AGED
97 YEARS

HERE LYETH THE BODY OF
NICOLAS DE LA CHEROIS MAJOR
IN THE LORD LIFFORDS REGIMENT
OF FOOT DECEASED JUNE 15th 1702
AGED 53 YEARS. ALSO THE BODY OF
NICOLAS DE LA CHEROIS HIS SON
WHO DECEASED OCTOBER THE 22nd
1708 AGED 12 YEARS. ALSO THE
BODY OF MARY DE LA CHEROIS
WIFE OF SAID MAJOR DE LA CHEROIS
WHO DECEASED DECEMBER 22nd
1724 AGED 60 YEARS

10. Huguenot memorial in the graveyard at Lisburn Cathedral.

5 June 1646, and a well-preserved memorial in Clonfeacle Parish Church, Co. Tyrone, is mounted over the spot where he is buried. This battle, one of the few great Irish military victories over the English and Scots, was not followed up and a great opportunity to expel the settlers from Ulster was lost.

St Mary's Church in Kilkenny city was deconsecrated in the late twentieth century and today serves a variety of social purposes. What was the north transept now contains a remarkable collection of monuments and memorials dating from the Middle Ages. The largest and most impressive, made of Kilkenny marble, rising in tiers to a height of fifteen feet and capped by a skeletal figure holding a scythe and hourglass, is that to Richard and Edward Rothe (died 1637) (sculptor: Patrick Kerin). In the sixteenth and seventeenth centuries tombs and monuments of this kind were usually commissioned during the lifetime of the deceased.

Another memorial worthy of mention is that to Mrs Abigail Handcock in St Mary's, Athlone, Co. Westmeath, with its open pediment, coat of arms and attractive lettering framed by pilasters. It was raised by her husband, William Handcock, following her death in 1680.

Huguenots (French Protestants) first arrived in Ireland in the middle of the seventeenth century; their numbers increased following the revocation of the Edict of Nantes in 1685 and again after the Williamite victories at Aughrim and the Boyne. Industrious, capable and innovative, they quickly made Ireland their home and played a leading role in trade, banking and politics. A case in point is Louis Crommelin (1652–1727), buried in the graveyard of Lisburn Cathedral, Co. Antrim, who, at the invitation of William of Orange, settled in that town and was responsible for the organisation and improvement of the linen industry in Ulster. Inside the cathedral, the Reverend Dubourdieu, another Huguenot, is commemorated by a bust on a sarcophagus (sculptor: John Smyth).

3. THE GEORGIAN ERA (1714–1830)

The Georgian era coincided with the golden age of the Anglo-Irish Ascendancy and ushered in a period of peace and prosperity after years of war and strife. Art and architecture flourished in many parts of the island and Dublin became the second city of the British Empire. The ruling class in what was considered a Protestant nation achieved a proud standard of civilisation. Thomas Packenham wrote that 'They had a style and a sense of pride, a pride of community, colonial nationalism of a sort, bigoted and narrow as it was, that set them apart from a mere English garrison taking its orders from London'. It was also a society that over-indulged in its pastimes and activities. 'All there is gaiety, pleasure, luxury and extravagance', wrote Arthur Young of Dublin in 1771.

Excess was the hallmark of the Ascendancy in life and death. Funerals were lavish affairs and there were strict, but not equitable, rules with regard to mourning. A wife was required to mourn for her husband for a year and six weeks, a husband for his wife for six months! Such matters were taken very seriously, as a letter from Jane Austen to Cassandra Austen in 1799 reveals: 'We met Dr Hall in such very deep mourning that either his mother, his wife, or himself must be dead'.

Memorials to the dead were designed to emphasise the importance and high social standing of the deceased, while the epitaphs stressed their personal qualities, goodness and piety. In the age of the Grand Tour the classical style was *de rigueur* and perfectly reflected how they wished to be remembered. Certain symbols denoting death are employed on most memorials: the draped urn, the inverted torch, the veiled and weeping wife, the disconsolate husband, winged cherubs, putti (male and often obese children) and, for the military, the broken column, the riderless horse and the grieving comrades. Fine examples, often by the greatest sculptors of the age, are to be seen in many churches.

11. Sir Donough O'Brien and putto in Kilnasoolagh Church, Newmarket-on-Fergus, Co. Clare.

One of the most elaborate is that to Sir Donough O'Brien (1642–1717), the first of his line to embrace the Protestant faith, in Kilnasoolagh, Newmarket, Co. Clare. Homan Potterton describes it as 'theatrical and the most spectacular Irish example of the type of baroque art that one associates with 17th century Rome. The deceased, resplendent in contemporary costume, lies in meditation his hand under his cheek upon a rolled up mattress, his curly wig tumbling about his shoulders.' The complete monument, with winged cherubs and superbly carved Corinthian columns, is 5.5m high and was much admired in its day (sculptor: William Kidwell).

The monument to David la Touche in Delgany, Co. Wicklow, is even more impressive, being over 8m high and 5m wide. The marble life-size figure of the deceased stands on a pedestal at the point of a pediment with his wife close by, while his three sons, sitting on the base, are depicted as ancient Romans in attitudes of grief (sculptor: John Hickey). La Touche was the son of the Huguenot founder of the family bank, and he himself contributed £10,000 towards the foundation of the Bank of Ireland.

Another fine monument, but somewhat reduced because the base was removed in the nineteenth century, is that to Dr Marmaduke Coghill (1673–1738) in Drumcondra, Dublin

12. David la Touche and family in Christ Church, Delgany, Co. Wicklow.

(sculptor: Peter Scheemakers); the church was specifically built by his sister Mary to house it as the family vault in St Andrew's Church was not sufficiently spacious. Coghill was lord chancellor of Ireland, and one of his most famous judgements from the bench is recorded in the correspondence of Dean Swift. 'A case was brought before him wherein a man was sued for beating his wife. When the matter was agitated Coghill gave it as his opinion that although a man had no right to beat his wife unmercifully, yet, with such a little cane or switch as he then held in his hand, a husband was at

15

13. Dr Marmaduke Coghill in Drumcondra Church, Dublin.

liberty, and indeed invested with the power, to give his wife a moderate correction.' At the time Coghill was engaged to be married, but his fiancée broke off the engagement and he died a bachelor!

An imposing monument in St Mary's, Doneraile, Co. Cork, commemorates Lord Doneraile (1657–1727), a member of the St Leger family that founded the famous horse race of the same name in 1776. The memorial, roughly 4m tall by 2.5m wide, consists of a portico supported by marble pillars in which is enshrined a life-

14. Detail from the memorial to Lord Doneraile at St Mary's, Doneraile, Co. Cork.

size figure of Hope, holding an anchor in her right hand and leaning on a medallion depicting the deceased (sculptor: Sir Henry Cheere).

The memorial to Lord Chief Justice Henry Singleton, who died in 1780, in St Peter's, Drogheda, Co. Louth, has been described by Homan Potterton as 'one of the most attractively positioned in Ireland'. It includes a bust of the deceased, two putti, an inscribed plaque and a figure of mourning Justice holding her scales (sculptor: John Hickey).

Directly opposite is a monument to John Ball (1753–1813), with a portrait bust and sarcophagus. Ball, a lawyer, also has a monument in St Patrick's Cathedral. Both were sculpted by John Smyth.

15. John Ball in St Peter's, Drogheda, Co. Louth.

George Ogle (1742–1814), who represented County Wexford in parliament for 28 years, is remembered by a portrait statue in St Patrick's Cathedral (sculptor: John Smyth). The inscription refers to him, *inter alia*, as 'a perfect model of that exalted refinement which in the best days of our country characterised the Irish gentleman'. His wife's memorial, with a weeping woman leaning on an urn, is in St Iberius's Church, Wexford. It was erected by her sister eight years after her death and a year after the death of her husband and is inscribed as follows:

SACRED
To the memory of MRS. ELIZABETH OGLE
Wife of the RIGHT HONOURABLE GEORGE OGLE.
A more than loved sister and a Faultless Friend.
Her mind was as Pure and Angelical
As her form was Beautiful.
If a human being could be perfect
She was perfect.
She was truly beloved and esteemed,
As she is universally lamented
By all those who knew her
And increasingly so by her ever Sorrowing Sister
Jane Moore
Who to indulge her unabated Grief
Erects this humble tribute
To her matchless worth.
In the month of June 1815.

There are two important monuments in Christ Church Cathedral by John van Nost the younger. The first, in the porch, is to Thomas Prior (1682–1751), a founder member of the Royal Dublin Society and its first secretary. The relief shows Prior introducing Ceres (the Roman goddess of the earth) to Hibernia. The second, in the crypt, is to John Bowes (died 1767), and shows a life-size figure of Justice leaning on a medallion portrait of the deceased. Bowes, as lord chancellor, was firmly opposed to any relaxation of the Penal Laws.

In the south transept is the memorial to Robert, earl of Kildare (1673–1743). The earl lies flat on top of a sarcophagus, while his grieving wife stands beside him supported by their only surviving daughter. At his feet, his hands clasped in despair, stands his son and heir. On the side of the monument is the Kildare crest, which includes a monkey, thought to have been responsible for saving the life of an infant of the family during a fire (sculptor: Sir Henry Cheere).

Two country churches hold important monuments that are classical in style and promise eternal life. The first, at St Sinan's, Tyrellspass, Co. Westmeath, is to George Augustus, earl of Belvedere (1738–1814), who is shown on his deathbed while a figure of Faith directs his gaze heavenward, where an angel awaits

16. Monument to Lord Chancellor John Bowes in the crypt of Christ Church Cathedral, Dublin.

him. At his feet is a kneeling female figure and, beside her, a pelican feeding its young—a symbol of Christ's sacrifice (sculptor: John Bacon the younger). The second, at Tashinny Church, Co. Longford, is in memory of Judge Gore (died 1753) and quite different to any so far described. It shows the deceased rising from his tomb and gazing upwards, neither dead nor alive but in a state of transition, about to leave this world for the next (sculptor: John van Nost).

The memorial in Christ Church, Castlebar, Co. Mayo, commemorating Sir Henry Byngham (died 1714) and his wife Lettis (died 1728) was badly damaged when part of the wall to which it was attached collapsed, but it has since been partially restored. It includes two fine medallion portraits of Byngham and his widow that fortunately survived unharmed. The sculptor of the Byngham memorial is unknown, and this is also the case with the excellent monument to Marcus Beresford, earl of Tyrone (died 1763), and his wife Catherine (died 1769) at Holy Trinity, Clonegam, Co. Waterford. Two fine busts of the earl and his wife, within a marble frame, are watched over by two very large weeping putti on either side of an elongated urn.

The epitaphs of the period often praised the qualities of the deceased to a degree that is almost laughable today; most portray people who are paragons of virtue. That this was not always the

17. *Detail from the monument to the earl of Belvedere at St Sinan's, Tyrellspass, Co. Westmeath.*

case has been proven by Étain Murphy in her fine book *A glorious extravaganza*, and one can have similar doubts about James Hamilton, whose monument with medallion portrait is in Holmpatrick Church, Skerries, Co. Dublin:

18. *Judge Gore rising from his tomb at Tashinny, Co. Longford.*

19. *Monument to Mary Anne Rossmore in St Patrick's, Monaghan.*

20. *Sir Henry Byngham and his second wife Lettis in Christ Church, Castlebar, Co. Mayo.*

21. *The earl and countess of Tyrone and putti in Holy Trinity, Clonegam, Co. Waterford.*

In Memory
Of James Hamilton of Sheep Hill in this County
late Proprietor of this Manor
A GENTLEMAN
who during a long and most active life
displayed that zealous energy and ingenuous integrity
that form the Useful and the Virtuous man
His Mind
was vigorous temperate and discerning
His heart
warm, liberal and sympathetic
He died on the 20th October 1800
In the 73rd year of his age
with that Humble Firmness and Placid confidence
that attend the close
of a virtuous and religious life.
Of the uncommonly numerous offspring
of thirty six children
He was survived by eight sons and eight daughters
who in his death have to lament
the absence of a cheerful and confidential Friend
as well as the removal
of the most anxious and solicitous
of parents.

An extract from a memorial in Templederry Parish Church, Co. Tipperary, typifies how members of the Ascendancy viewed themselves and the manner in which they related to those they considered their inferiors:

Sacred to the memory of
Thomas Otway Esquire
of Castle Otway and Lissen Hall.
At the latter residence he breathed his last
on the 26th day of June 1786 in the 56th year of his age.
Sincerely regretted by his equals
(superiors he had none)
and followed to the tomb by thousands of the labouring poor
with tears and lamentations.

22. *Memorial to the earl and countess of Aldborough at St Mary's, Baltinglass, Co. Wicklow.*

The memorial to the 4th earl of Massereene, who died in 1816, in All Saints Parish Church, Antrim, is a fine example of the work of John Flaxman, one of England's greatest sculptors. It has standing figures, representing the earl's wife and daughter, on either side of the epitaph, a theme that the artist frequently repeated.

Pride and social standing are characteristic of all these monuments, but there is an absence of sentiment and true feeling. A different type of memorial emerges in the early nineteenth

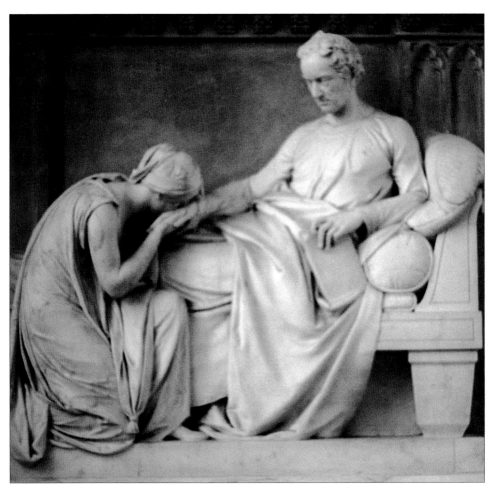

23. Monument to John James Maxwell, earl of Farnham, in Urney Parish Church, Cavan.

century, however, in which allegory plays no part and the main emphasis is on personal grief. This is epitomised by a relief commemorating Lady Mary Anne Rossmore, who died in 1807, in St Patrick's, Monaghan. Entitled 'The Parting Glance', it shows Lady Rossmore on her deathbed being visited for the last time by her mourning husband. He is being restrained by his son, while the family dog howls in sympathy (sculptor: Thomas Kirk). Lord Rossmore recovered from his loss and his second wife, Lady Augusta Rossmore, who died in 1840, is commemorated in the same church. Her simple but beautiful and touching memorial, entitled 'The Vacant Chair', shows his lordship seated in an attitude of despair beside his wife's vacant chair (sculptor: Lewis of Cheltenham).

The very fine monument to John James Maxwell, earl of Farnham (1759–1823), in Urney Parish Church, Cavan town, has a

24. *Late Georgian gravestone at St John's, Ballymore Eustace, Co. Kildare.*

similar theme. It shows him on his deathbed while his wife kneels beside him, holding his hand and drawing it to her lips. The figures are beautifully sculpted and the sense of impending loss touchingly expressed. It cost 1,000 guineas in 1826 (sculptor: Sir Francis Chantrey).

Only the wealthy could raise monuments of the type described above, and memorials to people of modest means are rare. There is, however, a touching example in Aghavea Church, near Brookeborough, Co. Fermanagh, with the following epitaph inscribed on a plain stone slab:

To the memory of
Richard Tribe
Son of Maria Sterne
by a former husband
a most lovely and engaging boy

25. *A typical eighteenth-century grave at St Brigid's, Stillorgan, Co. Dublin.*

who was killed near this church
in the presence of
his afflicted mother
by the overturning of a jaunting car
May 1812

A rare example of humour is the epitaph on the tombstone of John Edwin, who is buried in the graveyard of St Werburg's, Werburg Street, Dublin. Edwin was an actor at the Crow Street Theatre and his death was blamed on a mixture of grief and annoyance after he received a bad review:

26. *Mrs Susanna Mason and putto in Waterford Cathedral.*

27. *Mrs Jane Hamilton ascending into heaven at Ballykelly, Co. Londonderry.*

'Tis strange the mind, that very fiery particle,
Should let itself be snuffed out by an article.

Memorials raised solely to women are fairly rare. That to Elizabeth la Touche (1757–1842) in Christ Church, Delgany, Co. Wicklow, is a fine marble plaque with epitaph and urn on a black background. A similar monument with inverted torches is in St Sinan's, Tyrellspass, Co. Westmeath, and commemorates Jane, countess of Belvedere, who died in 1836. The epitaph on the latter refers, *inter*

28. Bagnel Gurly in St Mary's, Carlow.

This Monument was Erected by
THO.ˢ GURLY ESQ.ᴿᴱ.
as an affectionate Tribute to the Memory of his Brother
BAGNEL GURLY ESQ.ᴿᴱ.
and to Commemorate his many Virtues.
His Friends and acquaintance lament the irreparable Loſs
of his Sincere and warm Friendship.
Agreeable and instructive Conversation.
polite and Chearful Manners
Liberal yet prudent Hospitality and
every Social Virtue that sweetens and adorns private Life
he Died on the 25.ᵗʰ day of February 1796
in the 25.ᵗʰ Year of his Age.

alia, to 'her masculine understanding and unvaried maternal solicitude and care'.

An attractive memorial in Waterford Cathedral remembers Mrs Susanna Mason, who ran a well-known girls' school in the city and died in 1752 'after a life of exemplary piety'. Her medallion portrait, on which a weeping putto leans, depicts a woman of strong character and determination (sculptor: John van Nost).

The memorial to Mrs Jane Hamilton (died 1716) in Tamlaght Finlagan Parish Church, Ballykelly, Co. Londonderry, is probably unique in Ireland. This has an effigy of the deceased kneeling on a cushion and about to be crowned by two hovering cherubs holding a 'Crown of Glory'. On either side sit grieving putti (sculptor unknown).

31

IN MEMORY OF
TREVOR CORRY, KNIGHT,
YOUNGEST SON OF
ISAAC AND CÆZAREA CORRY OF NEWRY.
HE WAS MANY YEARS BRITISH CONSUL
AT DANTZIG,
WAS CREATED BARON OF THE KINGDOM
OF POLAND
BY STANISLAUS AUGUSTUS IN 1773,
AND DIED AT PIRYTZ IN POMERANIA 1. SEP. 1781.

THOUGH LONG A RESIDENT IN A FOREIGN LAND,
HE FORGOT NOT THE WANTS OF HIS OWN.
HE WAS THE FIRST WHO SUGGESTED THE NECESSITY
FOR A NEW CHURCH IN HIS
NATIVE TOWN,
TOWARDS WHICH PURPOSE HE BEQUEATHED
1000 POUNDS. 37 YEARS BEFORE THE ERECTION
OF THIS PRESENT CHURCH OF ST MARY'S
HE ALSO LEFT 5000 POUNDS TO THE
POOR OF NEWRY.

29. St Mary's, Newry, Co. Down.

30. Eighteenth-century tomb of Benjamin Woolley, his son and daughter and eleven members of the Truell family at St Thomas's, Wicklow.

TO THE MEMORY OF
BENJAMIN WOOLLEY OF EASTSHEEN
IN THE COUNTY OF SURRY ESQ
WHOSE REMAINS WITH THOSE OF HIS SON CHARLES
AND OF HIS DAUGHTER KATHARINE ARE HERE DEPOSITED
THIS MONUMENT WAS ERECTED
AT THE DESIRE OF HIS DAUGHTER MARY
BY HER HUSBAND ROBERT MARSHALL ESQ
FOR MANY YEARS ONE OF THE JUSTICES OF THE
COURT OF COMMON PLEAS IN THIS KINGDOM
IN THE YEAR
1768.

To close this chapter, three other attractive memorials deserve mention: first, one in St Mary's, Carlow, to Bagnel Gurly, who died, aged 24, in 1796 (sculptor: Richard Morrison); second, the memorial of the earl and countess of Aldborough in St Mary's, Blessington, Co. Wicklow (made to the design of John Bacon the Elder); and third, that in St Mary's, Newry, Co. Down, to Trevor Corry, who was British consul in Danzig (now Gdansk) for many years and died in Poland in 1781 (sculptor: William Spence). All three typify the fine workmanship and good taste of this remarkable period in Ireland's cultural history.

4. THE VICTORIAN ERA (1837–1901)

Queen Victoria (1819–1901) reigned for over 60 years, and her sense of duty, strict moral code and family values came to symbolise the ethos of the second half of the nineteenth century in both Great Britain and Ireland. In a period of religious revival, the Gothic replaced the Classical as the preferred style of church-building and ornamentation and, encouraged by Augustus W. N. Pugin (1812–52) and his followers, came to be viewed as the only true Christian architecture. The change was gradual, however, and in the first half of the nineteenth century Classical monuments continued to be popular but less grandiose, with greater emphasis on the Christian virtues and the hope of reunion in the life to come. Biblical quotations were increasingly incorporated and became a feature of most memorials over the next hundred years.

The monument in Monkstown to Richard Browne, who died in 1838, has two weepers leaning on a column and incorporates Classical symbols. Underneath are the words 'Sorrowing but not as others who have no hope' (sculptor: Thomas Kirk). The monument in Finglas to William Gregory, who died in 1853, has a finely sculpted weeper holding a laurel wreath. His epitaph records that the last words he spoke were 'Lord Jesus receive my spirit'.

There is a weeper holding an anchor on the monument in St Mary's Cathedral, Limerick, to Robert Maunsell Gabbett, who died in 1850. His epitaph ends with the words 'Mark the perfect man and behold the upright for the end of that man is peace'.

A later Classical monument is that in Waterford Cathedral to Joseph Makesy, who died in 1868. It is a charming memorial and depicts an angel unveiling a medallion portrait of the deceased (sculptor: Samuel Lynn).

Despite the Act of Union and Catholic Emancipation in 1829, the Ascendancy still held sway. At a time when funerals were occasions of great pomp and ceremony, no expense was spared in providing suitable memorials to the dead commensurate with their

31. Greek Revival memorial to Richard Brown at Monkstown Parish Church, Co. Dublin.

IN A VAULT BENEATH THIS CHURCH
REST THE REMAINS OF THE LATE
RICHARD BROWN ESQ^R
WHO DEPARTED THIS LIFE
OCT^R 16TH A.D 1838
LAMENTED IN DEATH AS IN LIFE BELOVED
ESPECIALLY
BY THE CHILDREN WHO AFFECTIONATELY
DEDICATE THIS TABLET TO HIS MEMORY

"Sorrowing but not as others who have no hope."

social position in life. Many show the deceased in a recumbent position, and one of the most beautiful but saddest is that in Holy Trinity, Clonegam, Co. Waterford, to Florence Grosvenor (1840–73), wife of the 5th marquess of Waterford, who died in childbirth. Carved out of white marble, she is seen on her deathbed holding her stillborn son (sculptor: Sir Joseph E. Boehm). Kiltennel Church, Co. Wexford, houses a similar beautiful recumbent effigy of Charlotte, countess of Courtown, who died at the age of 29 (sculptor: Thomas Campbell).

32. A typical early Victorian memorial in Limerick Cathedral.

The monument to the wine merchant and member of parliament Nathaniel Sneyd in Christ Church Cathedral is considered the finest work of the sculptor Thomas Kirk and shows the deceased on his deathbed. He died in 1833 when he was shot in a Dublin street by 'an unhappy maniac' who happened to be the brother of a local clergyman. Sneyd is also remembered by a plaque in Cavan Parish Church.

A lovely monument in the chancel of St Peter's, Kiltegan, Co. Wicklow, remembers Margaret B. Hume of Humewood Castle. She is shown on her deathbed, watched over by her grieving husband and two children (sculptor: Steinhauser of Rome, 1871). Further tragedy was to follow as the survivors died soon afterwards, the

33. *The marquise of Waterford, Florence Grosvenor, and her still born son at Holy Trinity, Clonegam, Co. Waterford.*

34. *Tomb of Charlotte, countess of Ross, in Kintennel Church, Co. Wexford.*

35. *Detail from the monument to Nathaniel Sneyd MP in the crypt of Christ Church Cathedral, Dublin.*

36. *Memorial to Margaret Hume in St Peter's, Kiltegan, Co. Wicklow.*

37. *The earl of Belfast and his mother in Belfast City Hall.*

husband aged 30 and the children four and nine respectively. A third child died in infancy.

A recumbent monument to the earl of Belfast shows him being consoled by his mother as he lies gravely ill with the consumption from which he died in 1853, aged 26. In Homan Potterton's view, 'this is certainly the most beautiful Victorian monument in Ireland and the quality of the carving raises it above pure Victorian sentimentality, resulting in an exquisitely moving composition'. Originally housed in a private chapel in the grounds of Belfast Castle, it has found a new home in Belfast City Hall (sculptor: Patrick MacDowell).

38. Lady Emily Hughes in St Iberius's, Wexford.

Giving birth in the nineteenth and earlier centuries was full of danger. A memorial bust of Lady Emily Hughes in St Iberius's, Wexford, relates how she died in childbirth at the age of 27 in 1868, while her baby boy died three months later. Infant mortality was also commonplace. A wall monument in Donaghmore Parish Church, Co. Tyrone, remembers the three children of John Ynyr and Lady Caroline Burges, who died in 1840, 1845 and 1850 aged four, eleven and eight respectively. Another in Kilbride, Co. Wicklow, remembers the two children of Major and Mrs Gaynor, each of whom died at eleven years of age. A headstone in Killabban churchyard, Co. Laois, tells us that four children of William and Anne Smith died between 1838 and 1848, aged fifteen, six, two and eight months. Other examples abound.

39. Donaghmore Parish Church, Co. Tyrone.

40. St Michael's, Castlecaulfield, Co. Tyrone.

41. Monument to the 6th Viscount Massereene in All Saints Antrim.

The Gothic Revival in church architecture was paralleled by memorials in the same style. An imposing example in All Saints, Antrim, is that to the 6th Viscount Massereene, who died in 1863. Attached to the north wall and carved from Caen stone, it shows the deceased, recumbent in the robes of a Knight of St Patrick, under a High Victorian triple canopy (sculptor: J. R. Kirk).

Two other fine examples are by the sculptor Edward Richardson. The first, in St Peter's, Bandon, Co. Cork, is to the memory of James Bernard (1784–1856), 2nd earl of Bandon, whose full-length recumbent figure, dressed in his coronation robe

42. *Mrs Mary Beresford in Kilmore Cathedral.*

with hands clasping his sword, lies on a Gothic altar-tomb. The second, in St Canice's Cathedral, Kilkenny, remembers the marquess of Ormonde, who died in 1854, and was described at the time of its installation as 'a very beautiful altar tomb with recumbent effigy' by Rev. James Graves in his *History of St Canice's Cathedral, Kilkenny* (1857). It might be thought that eminent aristocrats of this kind would have noble deaths, but in fact Viscount Massereene died from the effects of a fall while uprooting a shrub in his garden, and the marquess of Ormonde suffered a stroke whilst swimming with his children at the seaside.

The great effect of the Gothic Revival on memorials was the renewed interest in stained glass. In 1800 only a handful of churches had coloured glass of any kind, but when Queen Victoria died in 1901 it was the most popular type of memorial, much of it

43 (left). James Boyle Bernard on horseback in Tuam Cathedral.

44 (right). Mary M. Stoney in Christ Church, Delgany, Co. Wicklow.

imported from Germany, England and France. As many as 50 local firms were also engaged in its manufacture, which gives some idea of the huge demand. Most such memorials commemorate members of the Ascendancy, local gentry, rich parishioners and the clergy, and, with few exceptions, have a biblical theme. Such subjects as 'The Good Samaritan', 'The Good Shepherd', 'Christ blessing little children', 'The Nativity' and 'The Ascension' were especially popular. The memorial to Mary M. Stoney in Delgany, Co. Wicklow, is unusual as it depicts the deceased, who died in 1898 at the age of fifteen, in her own likeness. A two-light window in memory of Major David Ruttledge (died 1886) in Tuam Cathedral, Co. Galway, shows him at prayer dressed as a Roman

45. *Memorial to Arthur, 5th marquess of Downshire, at St Malachi's, Hillsborough, Co. Down.*

centurion, and in the same church we see James Boyle Bernard (died 1884) on horseback in the role of St Martin of Tours as he divides his cloak with his sword and presents it to a beggar. These latter represent a muscular kind of Christianity that was popular at the time.

As the century progressed, memorials were raised to lesser mortals; for example, at St John the Evangelist, Killyleagh, Co. Down, we are reminded that John Henry Howe Lawther entered the Ulster Bank at an early age, served therein for eighteen years and died manager of Dromore Branch, Co. Tyrone, in 1883 aged 33.

Much more exotic is the memorial at St Catherine's, Ahascragh, Co. Galway, to Lawrence Kearns, who was private secretary to Queen Victoria's envoy in Abyssinia (now Ethiopia). Both were imprisoned and held in chains for five years by the Emperor Theodore until rescued in 1868 by a relief force commanded by Field Marshall Lord Napier. Kearns died three years later, aged 26, and is buried near Massowah on the Red Sea.

Sir Benjamin Lee Guinness (1798–1868), of the great brewing family, was lord mayor of Dublin in 1851 and Conservative MP for the city during the last three years of his life. It was thanks to his generosity that St Patrick's Cathedral was restored in 1865, and there is a fine, seated statue of him at the entrance to the south door, 'erected by his fellow countrymen in grateful remembrance' (sculptor: John H. Foley).

Arthur, 5th marquess of Downshire, who died in 1874, is remembered by a fine memorial in St Malachi's, Hillsborough, Co. Down. Underneath a curtain held aloft by two cherub heads is a medallion portrait of the deceased supported by two angels, while below kneel his wife and young son waving towards him (sculptor: J. Forsyth). His funeral was memorable, as during the tolling of the church bells the fifth bell of the peal cracked.

The greatest calamity to befall Ireland in the nineteenth century was the Great Famine of 1845–9, when over a million people died of hunger and disease and a further million emigrated. Despite the scale of the disaster, public monuments to its victims are not numerous and Church of Ireland memorials rare, although we know that clergymen and parishioners in the famine areas succumbed to its effects. A memorial in Christ Church, Castlebar, Co. Mayo, remembers Edward John Thomas White, paymaster and purser in the Royal Navy, who died of fever 'caught in discharge of a special duty distributing seed for the government to the distressed peasantry of Mayo on the 25th July in the year of famine 1847'. A wall-tablet in St Patrick's, Kenmare, Co. Kerry, commemorates the life and service to the community of Dr George Mahony Mayberry, who died in 1880, and recalls how 'he tended the sick and dying throughout the years of famine and distress in the surrounding districts'. A memorial was erected in 1996 by Kildorrery Historical Society 'in memory of those who died in the Great Famine 1845/7' and is situated in a corner of the graveyard of St Colman's, Farahy, Co. Cork.

46. Great Famine memorial at St Colman's, Farahy, Co. Cork.

While not strictly a memorial, the 'Briddock plaque' in St Patrick's Cathedral, Trim, Co. Meath, is of considerable interest and, possibly, unique in Ireland because it is a clause from the will, dated 1854, of Robert Briddock, a Dublin merchant. Mr Briddock left funds from which a suit of clothes, shirts, shoes and the like were to be provided for poor male parishioners in Trim. A sum was

IN LOVING MEMORY OF
Mʀ S.W. GORDON
of 3 Blackhall Street,
WHO FROM BOYHOOD EARNESTLY PROMOTED
THE INTERESTS OF THESE PARISHES
AS VESTRYMAN, SYNODSMAN, NOMINATOR,
MEMBER OF THE CHOIR AND SCHOOLBOARD,
AND CAPTAIN OF THE BICYCLE CLUB.
HE ENTERED INTO REST
ON 25ᵀᴴ MARCH 1901, AGED 46,
"IN SURE AND CERTAIN HOPE."

47. Tablet in St Werburg's, Dublin.

Sacred to the memory
of
JOHN MULGRAVE,
an African Boy, Shipwrecked in
a Spanish Slave Ship on the
Coast of Jamaica in the Year 1833,
when he was taken under the protection
of the EARL of MULGRAVE,
then Governor of that Island,
in whose family he resided
till the 27 of February 1838, when
it pleased God to remove him from
this life by a severe attack of
Small Pox.

His Integrity, Fidelity, and kind
and amiable qualities, had endeared
him to all his Fellow Servants, at
whose desire this Tablet is erected
by his Godmother.

48. Tablet in St Werburg's, Dublin.

also set aside to pay for young boys to be apprenticed to the woollen industry, each to be provided with a Bible and a Book of Common Prayer. All of the recipients had to be Protestant, and to ensure entitlement the males had to be in constant attendance at noon services in church in their Briddock dress! The fund, which started with a sum of £500 sterling, lasted until 1920.

5. MAUSOLEUMS

The mausoleum is the supreme funerary monument and derives its name from the great tomb (one of the Seven Wonders of the Ancient World) erected by Queen Artemesia for her consort-brother Mausolus at Halicarnassos in Asia Minor (modern-day Turkey) in the fourth century BC. All roofed and free-standing buildings erected as a memorial and permanent home for the dead or their ashes are named after this structure. Most are of sturdy construction, classical in style, conspicuous and designed to make the greatest possible impact on posterity. As the Roman poet Ausonius reminds us, however, 'death comes even to the monumental stones and the names described thereon'.

Ireland has a surprisingly large number of mausoleums, and three of the finest are at Knockbreda Parish Church on the outskirts of Belfast. They were erected at the end of the eighteenth century by wealthy families of the city, some of whom had trading links with India. All are square in plan and have elegant arrangements of columns and pilasters with superstructures of pyramids, obelisks and urns. The two most elaborate are those of the Greg and Cunningham families, while the Rainey tomb, of the same period, is perfectly proportioned and crowned by four pyramids at each corner. These mausoleums appear to be by the same hand but the name of the architect is not known. All are showing their age and there must be some concern for their future.

Not far away, in the grounds of St Elizabeth's Church, Dundonald, is the Cleland mausoleum, one of the largest and most attractive in Ireland, erected by Eliza Cleland in memory of her husband, Samuel Cleland, who died in 1842. It consists of an underground vault with a neo-classical superstructure which is the pedestal for the cupola supported by Ionic columns. Overall it is not unlike the tower and cupola of St Stephen's Church, Upper Mount Street, Dublin, built a few decades earlier.

49. Greg memorial at Knockbreda Parish Church, Co. Down.

Probably the largest mausoleum in Ulster, with a frontage of four Tuscan columns supporting the pediment, is in the churchyard of St Michael's Church, Castlecaulfield, Co. Tyrone. It was erected in 1822 by the Burges family.

The pyramid is a popular roofing feature, and the mausoleum at Kilbixy churchyard, Co. Westmeath, is a good example. Here a steep-sided stone pyramid rests on a solid stone box with Doric columns. Inside are three sarcophagi containing the remains of various members of the Malone family, including Lord Sunderlin. The earliest death recorded is that of Anthony Malone, who died in 1776, but in James Howley's opinion the likely date of construction is the second decade of the nineteenth century.

50. Cleland mausoleum at St Elizabeth's, Dundonald, Belfast.

Similar pyramid-roofed structures can be found in other parts of Leinster, as in the churchyard of St John the Baptist, Hacketstown, Co. Carlow. There, the mausoleum was erected in 1844 by Christiana Hozier for her mother, also Christiana, and her father James, who died in 1825 and 1844 respectively. Built entirely of granite, it looks almost indestructible.

The mausoleum at St Mary's, Baltinglass, Co. Wicklow, is also built of granite but the pyramid does not cover the entire roof as at Hacketstown. It was erected in 1832 by Lord Aldborough in memory of the Stratford family.

The Westby family mausoleum at St Peter's, Kiltegan, Co. Wicklow, also topped by a small granite pyramid, is completely overshadowed by the nearby unusually large stone-roofed Hume mausoleum built by James Brooks about 1866. The latter is

51. Hozier
mausoleum at St
John the Baptist's,
Hacketstown, Co.
Carlow.

52. Entrance to
Westby mausoleum
at St Peter's,
Kiltegan, Co.
Wicklow.

53. Memorial to Mary Tighe at Inishtioge, Co. Kilkenny.

54. Barrymore mausoleum at Castle Lyons, Co. Cork.

55. *Lord Portarlington's mausoleum at St John's, Coolbanagher, Co. Laois.*

56. *McClintock mausoleum, Drumcar churchyard, Co. Louth.*

described by Maurice Craig as 'very grand' and by Jeremy Williams as 'the most bombproof of Ireland's mausolea'.

A notable granite-built mausoleum in the churchyard of St Mary's, Inistioge, Co. Kilkenny, was erected in memory of the poetess Mary Tighe (1772–1810). Inside is a full-length recumbent effigy of the deceased by John H. Flaxman.

The 10m-tall granite vault adjoining the graveyard at Kinnity Church, Co. Offaly, is the largest of the pyramid type in Ireland but also one of the least attractive. Six members of the Bernard family, who lived in nearby Castle Bernard, are interred within.

The impressive Barrymore mausoleum in Castle Lyons graveyard, not far from Fermoy, Co. Cork, is one of the few built of brick and has a central 'Venetian' opening with a pediment above.

It contains a fine monument in Italian marble (*c.* 1753) to James Barry, 4th earl of Barrymore, and was sculpted by David Sheehan. The old church at Castle Lyons has long since been abandoned and only the ruins remain, but the whole setting is very evocative and worth a visit.

The Dunraven mausoleum in the western wall of the cloisters in the old Augustinian abbey adjoining St Nicholas's Church, Adare, Co. Limerick, features a brick interior and was built in 1826. Jeremy Williams describes it as 'a minor masterpiece'.

There are only a small number of mausoleums whose architect's name is known for certain. One of these is at Coolbanagher, Co. Laois, where the church and adjoining mausoleum are the work of James Gandon (1743–1823). It was built for his friend and patron Lord Portarlington, who died in 1798, and is tucked away at the rear of the church and unusual for not being at all conspicuous.

There are two possible architects for the hexagonal Gothic Revival mausoleum at Drumcar Churchyard, Co. Louth, erected in memory of the McClintock family in the late nineteenth century. Jeremy Williams attributes it to Slater and Carpenter, while Maurice Craig thinks that it may be by J. F. Fuller. It is an interesting, heavily buttressed building, unlike any other of its kind in the country.

All of the mausoleums described above commemorate members of the aristocracy, rich merchants and landed gentry. The one at St Mary's, Marmullane, Passage West, Co. Cork, however, was raised in memory of Edward Daniel Brown, aged twenty, who was drowned in Passage West harbour in 1857. It is an attractive monument of modest size; each side of the entrance is flanked by a pair of Corinthian columns, while a recumbent angel lies in the arch overhead. His epitaph, engraved on the door, describes his many attributes, not least his kindness to the poor.

57. Monument to Edward Daniel Brown at Marmullane churchyard, Passage West, Co. Cork.

6. THE CLERGY

Memorials to clergymen are, as one would expect, commonplace and commemorate a variety of famous and interesting men.

On 3 April 2005 a special service was held in St Patrick's Cathedral, Dublin, to mark the 400th anniversary of the death of Archbishop Adam Loftus (1533–1605), who had a remarkable career in church and state and is buried with his wife and sixteen of their descendants in the Loftus family vault. Born in Yorkshire and an ardent Puritan, he was sent to Ireland in 1559 as chaplain to the lord deputy. Two years later, at the unprecedented age of 28, he was appointed archbishop of Armagh but was prevented by Shane O'Neill from moving to that city. He became dean of St Patrick's Cathedral in 1565 and archbishop of Dublin in 1567, and apparently held both posts until his death 40 years later. In 1578 he became lord high chancellor of Ireland, which powerful and influential political office he also held until he died. Loftus was largely responsible for having Trinity College built on its present site and was its first provost. He also built Rathfarnham Castle, Co. Dublin, as his private home. He was married to his wife Jane for 44 years and they had twenty children.

The graveyard opposite Kilmore Cathedral, near Cavan, Co. Cavan, contains the tomb of Bishop William Bedell (1571–1642). Born in England, he was at one time chaplain to the British ambassador in Venice, where he translated the Book of Common Prayer into Italian. He moved to Ireland in 1627 as provost of Trinity College, Dublin, and two years later was appointed bishop of Kilmore. In this capacity he felt it his duty to bring the Irish people within the Anglican fold, but realised at an early stage that little progress would be made if his clergy did not know the Irish language. He took steps to remedy this failing and became fluent himself. He then made the first translation of the Old Testament into Irish, assisted by two Roman Catholics, both of whom subsequently converted. Bishop Bedell was noted for his piety, learning and unselfishness, and his memory is still cherished in County Cavan. He died in 1642 as a result of the hardships he suffered during the 1641 rebellion. This was a period of the most bitter racial and religious strife, but such was the regard in which he was held by the general population that at his funeral a party of rebels formed a guard of honour and fired a musket volley over his grave. On the same day a Roman Catholic priest was heard to say 'May my soul be with Bedell's'. The present cathedral, built in the nineteenth century, was originally known as the 'Bedell Memorial Church'.

George Berkeley (1685–1753) is commemorated by a fine recumbent effigy (sculptor: Albert Bruce-Joy) in Cloyne Cathedral, Co. Cork, where he spent the last twenty years of his life as bishop. He is better known as one of the great scientific philosophers of the eighteenth century who founded the philosophical school of Immaterialism, which argued that the material world exists only in being perceived by the mind. In middle age he campaigned for a university in the American colonies to educate natives and colonists alike, and when the British government promised the then huge sum of £20,000 for this purpose he sailed for Rhode Island with his family. The money never arrived, however, and he returned, disillusioned, to Ireland and, eventually, to Cloyne. The University of California is named in his honour.

Reverend George Walker (1646–90) is famous as the heroic defender of Derry during the terrible 105-day siege in 1689. His reputation is largely based on his diary, published as 'a true account of the siege of Londonderry', but alternative sources claim that he did not give others sufficient credit and that his own role was exaggerated. He is remembered by stained glass windows in St Columb's Cathedral (an important defensive position close to the walls during the siege) and in a classical monument at St Michael's Church, Castlecaulfield, Co. Tyrone, where he was rector. He died serving as a chaplain at the Battle of the Boyne in 1690.

One of the most beautiful eighteenth-century memorials is that to Dean Peter Drelincourt (died 1720) in Armagh Cathedral. Greatly admired by the dean's contemporaries for its excellent likeness to the deceased, it is the work of John Michael Rysbrack. Homan Potterton describes the monument as 'an exquisite piece of workmanship'.

58. *Bishop Berkeley in Cloyne Cathedral.*

59. *Dean Peter Drelincourt in Armagh Cathedral.*

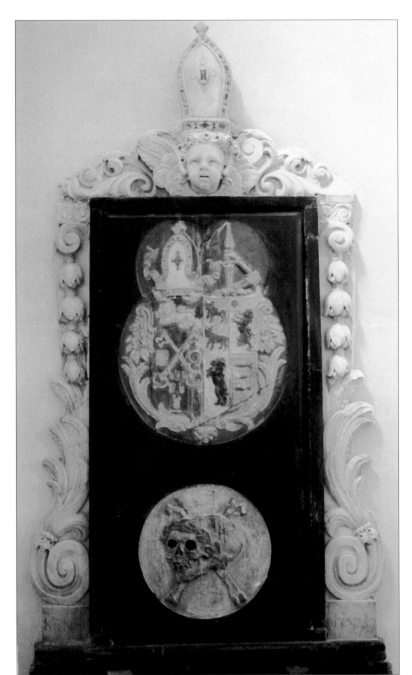

60. Memorial to Bishop Nathaniel Foy and his wife Frances in Waterford Cathedral.

The founder of Bishop Foy School, Bishop Nathaniel Foy (1645–1707), is commemorated in Waterford Cathedral by a memorial with skull and crossbones, winged cherub heads, coat of arms and bishop's mitre. Also remembered is his wife, Frances, who died in 1698 aged 95 (sculptor: William Kidwell).

61. Memorial to
the Reverend
Abraham Swan
(d. 1816) in a
grotto at Killurin
churchyard, Co.
Wexford.

Archbishop Narcissus Marsh (1638–1713) was, *inter alia*, provost of Trinity College, archbishop of Dublin and primate of all Ireland. He is best known, however, as the founder of Marsh's Library, Dublin, the oldest public library in Ireland, built in 1701. The interior has remained unchanged for 300 years and contains 25,000 books relating to the sixteenth, seventeenth and early eighteenth centuries. He is remembered by a large marble monument in St Patrick's Cathedral.

Dr Jonathan Swift (1667–1745), who served as dean of St Patrick's Cathedral, Dublin, for over 30 years, is probably Ireland's best-known clergyman. It is as a writer, social reformer, philanthropist and author of *Gulliver's travels* that he is chiefly remembered, however. He is also famous for his association with Hester Johnson ('Stella') and Esther Vanhomrigh ('Vanessa'). Swift is buried in St Patrick's and his epitaph, translated from the Latin, reads:

> 'Here is laid the body of Jonathan Swift, Doctor of Divinity, Dean of the Cathedral Church, where fierce indignation can no longer rend the heart. Go, traveller, and imitate if you can, this earnest and dedicated champion of liberty.'

He is also commemorated by a marble bust (sculptor: Patrick Cunningham) presented to the cathedral 30 years after his death. Stella is buried nearby. Less well known is the marble memorial to

his servant, also buried in the cathedral, the inscription on which
reads:

> 'Here lieth the body of Alexander McGee, servant to Dr Dean
> Swift of St Patrick's. His grateful master caused this monu-
> ment to be erected in memory of his discretion, fidelity and
> diligence in that humble station.'

Swift had originally intended to include the words 'and friend'
after 'servant', but this was considered inappropriate in the light of
their relationship and they were omitted.

Thomas Lewis O'Beirne (1747–1823), whose memorial is in St
Patrick's Cathedral, Trim, Co. Meath, was a most interesting man.
The son of a Roman Catholic farmer, he was sent to France to study
for the priesthood, but after a period of ill health in England he
became an Anglican and was ordained there in 1772. After four
years as a chaplain in the Royal Navy, he returned to Ireland and
in 1791 was appointed rector of Templemichael, Co. Longford,
where his brother was the parish priest! In 1795 he was secretary
and chaplain to the lord lieutenant, and in 1798 became bishop of
Meath, a post he held until his death 25 years later. He was a bril-
liant administrator, and during his bishopric presided over the
building of no less than 72 glebe houses and 57 churches.

Archdeacon John Elgee (1753–1823), whose granddaughter
Jane ('Speranza') was the mother of Oscar Wilde, is remembered
by a plaque in St Iberius's Church, Wexford. He narrowly escaped
death during the 1798 rebellion when a party of rebels burst into
the church whilst he was taking a service; not long afterwards he
attended Church of Ireland members of the United Irishmen who
were hanged on Wexford Bridge. These included Bagenal Harvey,
Cornelius Grogan and Dr John Colclough. His son, Richard
Waddy Elgee, founded the YMCA and was rector of St Iberius's
from 1843 to 1865.

The Reverend Samuel Haughton (1821–97), who is buried in
the family plot at Killeshin Church, Co. Carlow, was professor of
geology at Trinity College, Dublin, when he decided to study med-
icine and only later was ordained into the Church of Ireland.
Amongst his many interests, Haughton, of Quaker stock and
deeply religious, was concerned that many criminals sentenced to
death by hanging suffered far more than was necessary because
they did not die instantly but were more often suffocated at the end

of a short rope. In 1866, with his new medical knowledge, he calculated that a person weighing 160 pounds would have to be dropped 14ft to break his or her neck. Following publication of his calculations for various body weights and his recommendation for a more humane approach, his views were accepted by the authorities. Thereafter, criminals faced what became known as the 'long drop' and were sure of a speedy dispatch. Haughton also produced the first reasonable estimate of blood pressure and was a pioneer in the study of tides and currents.

Charles Inglis (1734–1816) was born in Ireland but went to Canada as a missionary for the Society for the Propagation of the Gospel in Foreign Parts at the age of 25. He spent the remainder of his life in that country and became bishop of Nova Scotia, the first bishop of a British colony. His brass memorial in St Patrick's Cathedral was placed there on behalf of churchmen in Nova Scotia, Delaware and New York; it describes him as 'one of the greatest among the many Irishmen who have served God under the Venerable Society' and as 'a fearless preacher of righteousness to his fellow colonists, to the heathen slaves and to the wandering tribes of Indians'.

There is a remarkable and beautifully sculpted memorial in Cloyne Cathedral, Co. Cork, to Bishop William Bennett (1745–1820), a zealous vice-president of the British and Foreign Bible Society. It portrays a handsome, almost naked, native of the Tropics kneeling under a palm tree, his hands clasped over a Bible and his gaze lifted heavenward as he embraces the faith (sculptor: James Heffernan).

The Reverend Arthur Bell Nicholls (1818–1906) was born in Killead, Co. Antrim. Following graduation from Trinity College, Dublin, his first curacy was at Haworth, Yorkshire, where Patrick Bronte (1777–1861), another Ulsterman and father of the famous Bronte sisters, Anne, Charlotte and Emily, was rector. Nine years later, in 1854, he married Charlotte, author of *Jane Eyre*, and they honeymooned in Ireland for a month. The marriage was happy but tragically short as Charlotte died the following year, leaving her father dejected and alone as his wife and all four children were now deceased. Nicholls looked after him until his death six years later and then returned to Ireland, where he lived for the rest of his life. He is buried at St Paul's Church, Banagher, Co. Offaly.

The Reverend James R. Stewart (1881–1916), who is remembered by a brass plaque in Monkstown Parish Church, Co.

62. Reverend William Bennett memorial in Cloyne Cathedral, Co. Cork.

SACRED TO THE MEMORY OF THE
RIGHT REVᴰ WILLIAM BENNETT, D.D.
FOR TWENTY SIX YEARS LORD BISHOP OF THE DIOCESE OF CLOYNE,
A MAN OF VARIED ATTAINMENTS, REFINED LITERARY TASTE,
SINGULARLY MODEST AND COURTEOUS IN MANNERS,
OF GREAT SIMPLICITY OF SPIRIT, AND GENUINE PHILANTHROPY OF HEART,
CALLED IN THE PROVIDENCE OF GOD
TO A HIGH AND RESPONSIBLE OFFICE IN THE CHURCH OF ENGLAND,
HE WAS ANXIOUS THAT SHE SHOULD MAINTAIN THAT DIGNIFIED POST IN THE DEFENCE
AND DISSEMINATION OF THE HOLY SCRIPTURES WHICH THE REFORMATION TAUGHT HER
TO OCCUPY, AND WHICH HER INTEREST AND DUTY ALIKE FORBID HER TO ABANDON,
HE, THEREFORE, DURING A PERIOD OF TEN YEARS
WAS A ZEALOUS VICE PRESIDENT OF THAT NOBLE INSTITUTION
THE BRITISH AND FOREIGN BIBLE SOCIETY,
ITS SACRED CAUSE WAS NEAR HIS HEART, ITS VINDICATION OPENED HIS LIPS,
AND DREW FROM THEIR CONCEALMENT TALENTS OF NO MEAN ORDER,
NOR WAS DEATH PERMITTED TO CLOSE HIS EYES UNTIL HE HAD WITNESSED
ITS UNPARALLELED SUCCESS UNDER THE MANIFEST BLESSING OF THE MOST HIGH.
HE RESIGNED HIS SPIRIT INTO THE HANDS OF HIS CREATOR ON THE 15ᵀᴴ DAY OF JULY 1820,
IN THE 74ᵀᴴ YEAR OF HIS AGE.

Dublin, was the son of the Reverend Robert W. and Louisa Stewart, both of whom were serving with the Church Missionary Society in China when they were murdered in 1895. Remarkably, despite this tragedy, he and four of his brothers and sisters later went to the same country as missionaries. When the Great War started, however, he felt that he must return to his compatriots in France, where he served as a chaplain in the Worcestershire Regiment. He

NEAR THIS PLACE ARE INTERRED THE REMAINS OF
THE RIGHT REVEREND THOMAS PERCY, D.D.
LORD BISHOP OF DROMORE,
TO WHICH SEE HE WAS PROMOTED IN MAY, MDCCLXXXII,
FROM THE DEANERY OF CARLISLE, IN ENGLAND.
THIS ELEVATED STATION HE FILLED NEARLY THIRTY YEARS,
RESIDING CONSTANTLY IN HIS DIOCESE,
AND DISCHARGING THE DUTIES OF HIS SACRED OFFICE
WITH VIGILANCE AND ZEAL;
INSTRUCTING THE IGNORANT, RELIEVING THE NECESSITOUS,
AND COMFORTING THE DISTRESSED, WITH PASTORAL AFFECTION,
REVERED FOR HIS EMINENT PIETY AND LEARNING,
AND BELOVED FOR HIS UNIVERSAL BENEVOLENCE,
BY ALL RANKS AND RELIGIOUS DENOMINATIONS,
HE DEPARTED THIS LIFE
ON THE XXXᵗ DAY OF SEPTEMBER, IN THE YEAR OF OUR LORD
MDCCCXI,
IN THE EIGHTY THIRD YEAR OF HIS AGE.

IN THE SAME GRAVE ARE DEPOSITED THE REMAINS
OF ANNE, HIS WIFE,
DAUGHTER OF BARTIN GOODRICHE, ESQᵗ OF DESBOROUGH
IN THE COUNTY OF NORTHAMPTON, ENGLAND;
WHOSE ESTIMABLE CONDUCT THROUGH LIFE,
RENDERED HER THE WORTHY PARTNER OF SUCH A HUSBAND.
SHE DIED ON THE XXXᵗ OF DECEMBER, MDCCCVI, AGED LXXIV YEARS.

THIS MEMORIAL OF DUTIFUL AFFECTION
IS INSCRIBED BY THEIR SURVIVING DAUGHTERS
BARBARA ISTED, AND ELIZABETH MEADE.

63. Bishop Thomas Percy memorial in Dromore Cathedral.

was killed there in 1916 while conducting a funeral service behind the front line.

An extremely sad memorial in St John the Evangelist's Church, Ardamine, Co. Wexford, records the death of the Reverend James S. Collins, another missionary with the CMS in China, who drowned there in 1897. A greater tragedy was to ensue the same year when, on their way home to Ireland, his wife Mary Isabella, his two-year-old daughter, one-year-old son and their nurse were lost in the wreck of the *Aden* in the Indian Ocean. Even sadder is an earlier memorial in Christ Church Cathedral with fine busts of

64. Memorial to Bishop Charles Warburton and his daughter in Cloyne Cathedral.

TO THE MEMORY OF
THE RIGHT REVD. CHARLES M. WARBURTON D.D
LORD BISHOP OF CLOYNE
DECEASED 9 TH AUGUST 1826 AGED 72 YEARS
AND OF SELINA WARBURTON
HIS AMIABLE AND BELOVED DAUGHTER WHO DIED 12 TH MARCH 1826 AGED 34 YEARS
THIS MEMORIAL OF AFFECTIONATE REGRET IS ERECTED BY HIS DISCONSOLATE WIDOW
FRANCIS WARBURTON AND CHILDREN
HE WAS CONSECRATED BISHOP OF LIMERICK 13 TH JULY 1815
AND TRANSLATED TO THIS SEE 20 TH SEPTEMBER 1820
TO A DIGNIFIED DEPORTMENT IN THE STRICT DISCHARGE OF HIS DUTIES
HE UNITED THE MOST ENGAGING SUAVITY OF MANNER
AND UNBOUNDED BENEVOLENCE

Bishop Welbore Ellis (died 1734) and his wife Diana (died 1739), which reminds us that seven of their eight children died before their second birthday (sculptor: possibly Joseph Nollekens).

A handsome tablet with marble mitre, crozier and Bible in Dromore Cathedral, Co. Down, commemorates Bishop Percy, a revered cleric who died in 1811 (sculptor: Sir Richard Westmacott). Also in the church are his vestments, displayed in a glass-fronted wardrobe in the choir.

A beautiful memorial with a figure of Grief kneeling before two draped urns in Cloyne Cathedral remembers Bishop Charles M. Warburton and his daughter Selina, both of whom died in 1826. The epitaph ends with the words: 'To a dignified deportment in

65. Memorial to the Reverend Robert Vicars in Coolbanagher Church, Co. Laois.

the strict discharge of his duties he united the most engaging suavity of manner and unbounded benevolence'.

Memorials depicting the Good Samaritan were popular in the eighteenth and early nineteenth centuries and were regarded as especially appropriate for doctors and clergymen. An attractive example in St John's, Coolbanagher, Co. Laois, is in memory of the Reverend Robert Vicars, curate and rector of the parish for many years, who died in 1829. It was erected 'by his Protestant parishioners and friends as a testimony of their sense of the many virtues of a man in whom was no guile' (sculptor: T. Kirk).

George Otto Simms (1910–91) was one of the outstanding Irish churchmen of the twentieth century, and as bishop of Cork and archbishop of Dublin and Armagh exercised great influence throughout the Church of Ireland and beyond. He combined scholarship with humility and goodness, and all who met him were struck by his spirituality, warmth and humour. He was a leading authority and lecturer on the Book of Kells, a fluent Irish-speaker and an ecumenist at a time when such ideas were not popular. His appointment as archbishop of Armagh in 1969 coincided with the outbreak of 'the troubles' in Northern Ireland; for a man of toler-ance and goodwill, but not a political prelate, this was a very trying time, during which he sought a peaceful and just solution to prob-

66. *Memorial window to the Reverend William Monk Gibbon in St Nahi's,*
Dundrum, Co. Dublin (artist: Catherine O'Brien).

67. *Detail from the memorial window to the Reverend Joseph Digges in Farnaught Church, near Mohill, Co. Leitrim (artist: Ethel Rhind).*

lems that appeared intractable. He travelled widely and was held in high esteem throughout the Anglican world and beyond. He is buried in the graveyard at St Maelruain's, Tallaght, Co. Dublin, and his memorial brass plaque in Christ Church Cathedral describes him as follows:

> Pastor — Leader — Scholar — Teacher
> Writer — Counsellor — Friend
> A man greatly loved.

7. SEAMEN

Although an island with a long coastline and a great ocean on its doorstep, Ireland, for a variety of reasons, does not have a great naval tradition. While memorials to seamen are not numerous, they are nevertheless always of interest.

Captain Robert Charles Halpin (1836–94), who is commemorated by a simple plaque in St Thomas's Church, Wicklow, went to sea at ten years of age and survived a shipwreck at sixteen. He quickly rose to officer rank and eventually became captain of Isambard Kingdom Brunel's *Great Eastern*, then the largest ship in the world. From it, in 1866, he laid the first transatlantic telegraph cable from Ireland to Newfoundland, and over the next ten years, from the same ship and in many different seas, succeeded in laying a total of 26,000 miles of cable. During all that time no member of his crew suffered serious injury. He retired at 40 to Tinakilly House (now a hotel) near Rathnew, Co. Wicklow, which is believed to have been paid for by a grateful British government. Many of the exhibits in the National Maritime Museum, Dun Laoghaire, Co. Dublin, including samples of the famous cables, belonged to Captain Halpin. In Holy Trinity Church, Castlemacadam, Co. Wicklow, there is an attractive marble memorial erected by Captain Halpin and the officers and crew of the *Great Eastern* to Robert Jones, assistant surgeon of that ship, who died in 1875, aged 23.

In the graveyard of the same church, a memorial to Captain James Thomas Belton of the steamship *City of Dundee* describes how 'by his devoted gallantry' he saved the lives of every passenger when his vessel was run into and sunk during a fog in Cardigan Bay on the morning of 4 October 1908. Captain Belton and two of his officers went down with their ship and 'shared the same glorious end'.

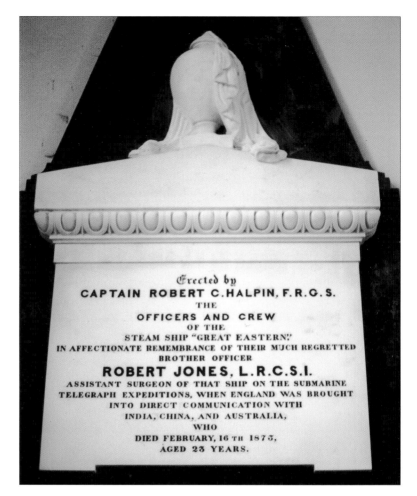

68. *Assistant surgeon Robert Jones in Holy Trinity, Castlemacadam, Co. Wicklow.*

Erected by
CAPTAIN ROBERT C.HALPIN, F.R.G.S.
THE
OFFICERS AND CREW
OF THE
STEAM SHIP "GREAT EASTERN."
IN AFFECTIONATE REMEMBRANCE OF THEIR MUCH REGRETTED
BROTHER OFFICER
ROBERT JONES, L.R.C.S.I.
ASSISTANT SURGEON OF THAT SHIP ON THE SUBMARINE
TELEGRAPH EXPEDITIONS, WHEN ENGLAND WAS BROUGHT
INTO DIRECT COMMUNICATION WITH
INDIA, CHINA, AND AUSTRALIA,
WHO
DIED FEBRUARY, 16 TH 1875,
AGED 23 YEARS.

There is a statue in St Patrick's Cathedral, Dublin, erected by the citizens of the city, to the memory of Captain John McNeill Boyd RN, commander of the coastguard vessel HMS *Ajax*, who also lost his life along with five members of his crew while on their way to help rescue the crew of the brig *Neptune*, which was wrecked on the rocks of the east pier at Kingstown (now Dún Laoghaire) during a fierce storm in February 1861. Other memorials to Boyd and his crew can be seen in Carrickbrennan churchyard (the old burial-ground of Monkstown Parish Church) and on the east pier at Dún Laoghaire, the latter erected by the members of the Royal St George's Yacht Club. In Derry Cathedral, Boyd is also remembered by a bas-relief in which he points seaward, instructing a seaman to throw a lifeline. The monuments in both cathedrals are by Sir Thomas Farrell.

TWO OF HIS OFFICERS
BOTH IRISHMEN
PATRICK HENRY LEBAN
SECOND OFFICER, AGED 45 YEARS.
AND
THOMAS BURKE
QUARTERMASTER, AGED 47 YEARS.
SHARED THE SAME GLORIOUS END
GOING DOWN WITH THE SHIP.

SACRED
TO THE MEMORY OF
CAPTAIN JAMES THOMAS BELTON
S.S. CITY OF DUNDEE,
BY WHOSE DEVOTED GALLANTRY ALL THE
PASSENGERS WERE SAVED, WHEN, DURING
A FOG, THE VESSEL WAS RUN INTO & SUNK
IN THE BAY OF CARDIGAN
EARLY ON THE MORNING OF 4TH OCT. 1909.

"WHEN THOU PASSEST THROUGH THE
WATERS, I WILL BE WITH THEE."

69.   Captain James Thomas Belton at Holy Trinity, Castlemacadam, Co. Wicklow.

77

70. *Memorial to Captain J. McNeill Boyd and his men in the old graveyard of Monkstown Church at Carrickbrennan, Co. Dublin.*

71. Tomb of Lieutenant Richard Roberts RN in Marmullane churchyard, Passage West, Co. Cork.

72. Master's mate Edward Percival RN in St Iberius's, Wexford.

73. *Midshipman James David Beresford RN in Ballykelly, Co. Londonderry.*

The small graveyard at Marmullane Church, Passage West, Co. Cork, is full of interest and includes the tomb of Lieutenant Richard Roberts, embossed with models of the sterns of each of the four ships in which he served. One of these was the *Sirius*, which he commanded when it became the first steamship to cross the Atlantic, arriving in New York harbour on 22 April 1838, after a voyage of nineteen days. The *Sirius* was propelled by two paddle-wheels and left Queenstown (now Cobh) with a crew of 35 and 450 tons of coal piled into every available space. The crossing passed uneventfully until the coal ran out in sight of the American coast, and it was only by burning all of the cabin furniture, wooden spars and one of the masts that they reached their destination. Only five hours after their arrival another of Brunel's ships, the much larger *Great Western*, steamed into New York but the glory went to the *Sirius*, which returned to Ireland in triumph. It is very strange that Roberts, whose title is given as captain in every description of his famous voyage, should have the lesser rank of lieutenant inscribed on his tomb.

In the eighteenth and nineteenth centuries life at sea was hard and dangerous, with accidents, harsh discipline and shipwrecks commonplace. Those who served on warships were exposed to greater perils. A dramatic monument in St Iberius's Church, Wexford, shows a longboat, crowded with sailors and with an officer waving his sword and hat, leaving the frigate HMS *Havannah* on its way to engage the enemy on the coast of Istria in Croatia. The date of the action was 6 January 1813, during the Napoleonic Wars, and the memorial remembers Edward Percival, a master's mate in the Royal Navy, who 'fell gallantly fighting his country's cause against an enemy of far superior force'. He was 21.

Lieutenant William Dobbs RN, son of the rector of Lisburn, whose wall memorial is in Lisburn Cathedral, Co. Antrim (sculptor: Edward Smyth), was married in the late 1770s during the American War of Independence. Soon afterwards, while he was staying at his family home near Carrickfergus, Co. Antrim, an American ship, the *Ranger*, sailed into Belfast Lough, and Dobbs, in the naval sloop HMS *Drake*, set out to do battle. In the ensuing engagement the sloop was boarded and captured and Dobbs was killed. Fortune did not favour him, as the captain of the American ship was John Paul Jones (1747–92), a very successful fighting sailor who today is regarded as the father of the United States navy.

*74. Surgeon
Henry George
Daniel RN in St
Iberius's, Wexford.*

In the eighteenth and early nineteenth centuries it was customary for boys to serve on warships, and Admiral Lord Nelson went to sea at the age of twelve. A memorial in Tamlaght Finlagan Church, Ballykelly, Co. Londonderry, describes the death of seventeen-year-old midshipman James David Beresford during the Napoleonic Wars. In December 1807, while his ship HMS *Phenix* was pursuing an enemy in a violent gale, he fell from the yard-arm and was drowned.

Death came in a variety of ways. Many parts of the world were unhealthy in the nineteenth century, and Henry George Daniel, surgeon on the HMS *Pioneer*, died of fever off the west coast of Africa (then known as 'the White Man's Grave') in 1879 at the age of 25. His attractive memorial, erected by the officers and crew of his ship, is in St Iberius's Church, Wexford.

There is a memorial showing two ships stranded in the Arctic ice in Seapatrick Church, Banbridge, Co. Down. It commemorates Captain Francis Crozier RN (1796–1848), a native of the town, and was erected some ten years after his death. Crozier joined the Royal Navy at fourteen, and after several Arctic and Antarctic voyages was appointed second in command to Captain Thomas Franklin, the commander of a high-profile expedition in 1845 whose purpose was to seek a north-west passage from the Atlantic to the Pacific. The expedition never returned, and it was not until 1859 that another Irishman, Captain Francis McClintock (1819–1907), discovered its fate. The two ships, *Erebus* and *Terror*, had been crushed by ice, and following Franklin's death Crozier took command. With about 100 survivors he tried to walk to the Canadian mainland but died in the attempt. Not one sailor lived to tell the tale, and the wrecks of the ships have never been found. The sculptor was Joseph R. Kirk, who was also responsible for the imposing monument to Crozier in the centre of Banbridge.

Another Arctic expedition followed in 1849, involving two ships, HMS *Enterprise* and HMS *Investigator*. The assistant surgeon of the former, Henry Mathias, died during the voyage, aged 28, and his marble monument, erected by brother officers, is in the crypt of Christ Church Cathedral. It shows the two ships surrounded by icebergs.

Admiral Robert Dudley Oliver (1766–1850) is commemorated by a brass plaque in Monkstown Parish Church, Co. Dublin, where he was buried. He was sent to sea at the age of thirteen in 1779, and soon afterwards, as a midshipman, saw action against the Spanish. One of his companions at the time was the future King William IV, known as 'the Sailor King'. In 1791, then a lieutenant, Oliver saved Francis Beaufort (the inventor of the Beaufort Scale) from drowning. Both were sons of clergymen. Subsequently, as a captain, he fought numerous engagements against the French during the Napoleonic Wars. He reported to Admiral Nelson at Portsmouth a few days before the latter left England prior to his death at the Battle of Trafalgar in 1805, but missed the action himself because of damage to his ship. He did, however, tow home some of the prizes. He retired with the rank of admiral and died at Dalkey in his 85th year.

One of those on board HMS *Victory* at Trafalgar was a young midshipman, Francis E. Collingwood, who is remembered by a tablet in St John's Church, Tralee, Co. Kerry.

Finally, in St Anne's Church, Strandhill, Co. Sligo is a particularly poignant memorial to James E.N. Wood of Woodville, Sligo, who died in 1859, aged 24, in the wreck of the *Admella* off the coast of New South Wales. Along with a mention of his father (also James) and mother Anne it concludes with the following touching verse:

> At length the longed for port I reach
> And glide from out the strife
> I need to gain Death's quiet beach
> To rest myself from Life.

8. ARTISTS, ARCHITECTS, MUSICIANS AND WRITERS

Many of Ireland's greatest writers and artists came from a Church of Ireland background but died abroad. George Bernard Shaw (1856–1950) and Seán O'Casey (1880–1964) were both cremated in Golders Green crematorium, London, whilst Oscar Wilde (1854–1900) and Samuel Beckett (1906–89) are interred at Père Lachaise and Montparnasse cemeteries, Paris, respectively. Sir William Orpen (1878–1931), the finest portrait-painter of his time, is buried in Putney Vale cemetery, London.

Probably the best-known grave in Ireland, visited by tens of thousands of tourists each year, is that of the poet and Nobel prizewinner William Butler Yeats (1865–1939), who is buried in Drumcliffe churchyard, Co. Sligo. The grave itself is plain and unadorned and the carving on the tombstone of indifferent quality, but the bleak epitaph, written by the poet, is one of the best-known in the English language:

'Cast a cold eye
on life, on death.
Horseman, pass by!'

There is no memorial to any member of the Yeats family in Drumcliffe Church, but Susan Mary Yeats is remembered by a bronze tablet in St John's Cathedral, Sligo, where she married John Butler Yeats (1839–1922), the celebrated painter, in 1863. They were the parents of W. B. Yeats, his famous painter brother Jack, and their two very talented sisters, Susan (Lily) and Elizabeth (Lolly), both of whom now rest in the same grave at St Nahi's churchyard, Dundrum, Co. Dublin. Also buried at St Nahi's is the poet and novelist William Monk Gibbon (1896–1987), son of a former rector. He left instructions that he was to wear his pyjamas,

75. *Sophia Fox,*
half-sister of
Maria Edgeworth,
in St John's,
Edgeworthstown,
Co. Longford.

SOPHIA FOX
1 March 1837.

SOPHIA
DAUGHTER OF R. L. EDGEWORTH ESQ.RE
BORN 27TH OF MAY 1803
MARRIED TO BARRY FOX ESQ.RE
1ST OF MARCH 1824
DIED 1ST OF MARCH 1837.

his most comfortable outfit, on the day of his interment.

Louis MacNeice (1907–63), the son of a Church of Ireland rector, has been described by Hugh Haughton (Senior Lecturer in English at the University of York) as 'one of the most various, prolific and influential Irish poets of the twentieth century with a particular impact on later poets from Northern Ireland where he was born'. In addition to his poetry, he wrote plays and travel books and worked for the BBC as a producer and writer. Cremated in London, he is remembered on the headstone of his mother's grave at Christ Church, Carrowdore, Co. Down, where his ashes rest. The poet Derek Mahon paid tribute to MacNeice in his poem 'In Carrowdore churchyard'.

Maria Edgeworth (1767–1849), the celebrated novelist, is buried in the Edgeworth family vault on the north side of St John's Church, Edgeworthstown, Co. Longford. She was a key figure in the development of the English novel and was admired by many of her contemporaries, including Sir Walter Scott, Lord Byron and Jane Austen, who sent her a copy of *Emma* on its publication in 1815. From 1800 until the appearance of Austen's *Sense and sensibility* in 1811 she was the most celebrated and successful of novelists writing in English. Her best-known work is *Castle Rackrent*, dealing with Irish regional life. There is a small, difficult-to-read tablet to her memory in the church, which also contains good memorials to her grandmother, Rachel Jane Edgeworth (1706–64), and her half-sister Sophia (1803–37). Her clever inventor father, Richard Lovell Edgeworth (1744–1817), to whom she was devoted, is buried beside her in the family vault. He was married four times and had 22 children, all of whom were schooled at home.

Oliver Goldsmith (1728–74), the poet, playwright and novelist, was born in County Longford but left Ireland when he was 28 to become an important figure in the literary London of his day. He produced such masterpieces as the novel *The Vicar of Wakefield*, the poem 'The Deserted Village' and the play *She stoops to conquer*. His father was curate at the church of St Munis, Forgney, Co. Longford, which contains a fine stained glass window to his memory. It was installed in 1897 by a group of admirers.

Edith Oenone Somerville (1858–1949) was not only a celebrated author but a musician, cattle-breeder, master of foxhounds and talented artist. Her greatest claim to fame is her authorship of *The Irish R.M.* and other stories in collaboration with her cousin Violet Florence Martin (Martin Ross), with whom she travelled widely and had a lifelong friendship. They are buried side by side in the graveyard of St Barrahane's Church, Castletownsend, Co. Cork, and commemorated in a delightful tablet on the north wall of the same church, designed by W. H. Sharpington and subscribed for by friends and admirers in America. Edith played the organ in St Barrahane's for 70 years and designed the mosaic floor in the

76. Oliver Goldsmith memorial window at St Munis's, Forgney, Co. Longford.

chancel in memory of Violet. She was also responsible for the installation of the beautiful Harry Clarke windows.

James Owen Hannay (1865–1950) is better known as George A. Birmingham, the *nom de plume* he used as author of more than 80 novels, plays and religious works. Much of his output concerned the antagonism between Catholic nationalists and Protestant unionists

FEAR GOD IN LIFE

In most grateful memory of
·EDITH ŒNONE SOMERVILLE, Hon. Litt. D.
·1858· – 1949.
· Author, Artist, Musician, M.F.H.
Her friends and admirers in America
have endowed the organ on which
she played for seventy years
and have raised this stone
to commemorate the one hundredth
anniversary of her birth.
To her name is joined, as she would
have wished, that of her beloved
cousin and collaborator
Violet Florence Martin (Martin Ross)
·1862 – ·1915··

77. Edith Oenone Somerville in St Barrahane's, Castletownsend, Co. Cork.

and was so controversial that he managed to alienate both groups; he eventually left Ireland and ended his days abroad. He was in a good position to write about such matters, having been deeply involved in the Gaelic League as a young man and later serving as a chaplain in the British army during the Great War. He is remembered by plaques in Christ Church, Delgany, Co. Wicklow, where he was curate from 1888 to 1892, and in Holy Trinity Church, Westport, Co. Mayo, where he was rector from 1892 to

1913.

The author Clive Staples Lewis (1898–1963) wrote on a variety of subjects but is best known for his books for children chronicling the land of Narnia. He came to the attention of a much wider audience when he and his wife, Joy Davidman, were portrayed in the film *Shadowlands*. He was baptised in St Mark's Church, Dundela, Co. Down, where his grandfather was rector, and there is a fine stained glass window in the nave presented by Lewis and his brother Warnie in memory of their father and mother (artist: Michael Healy).

Elizabeth Bowen (1899–1973), who has been described as the last of the Anglo-Irish novelists, is buried with her husband, Alan Charles Cameron, in the graveyard at Farahy Church, Kildorrery, Co. Cork. Close by is the site of 'Bowen's Court' (now demolished), which she inherited in 1930 and which was the title of an early novel dealing with the Anglo-Irish experience in twentieth-century Ireland. The latter was a favourite theme, as was loneliness, personal relationships and life in the London Blitz during the Second World War. She is remembered by a wall-tablet inside the church, where a memorial service is held in her honour every September.

Molly Keane (1904–96), who also wrote under the name M. J. Farrell, is another writer fascinated by the 'Big House' and the demise of the Protestant Ascendancy. She and her husband, Robert Keane, are buried in St Paul's churchyard, Ardmore, Co. Waterford.

Annie M. P. Smithson (1873–1948) was the most successful Irish romantic novelist of her day, with titles such as *The marriage of Nurse Harding* and *The Weldons of Tibradden*. She was brought up in a strict Dublin Church of Ireland family with a strong unionist tradition, but while serving as a Queen's nurse in Ulster as a young woman was so shocked by the political and religious divisions there that she converted to Catholicism and joined Sinn Féin. She tended the wounded during the 1922 Civil War, following which she was arrested and imprisoned. In later life she was a district nurse and did much to improve the lot of the nursing profession as secretary of the Irish Nurses' Union. Despite her change of religion and being disowned by most of her family, she was buried, at her own request, in Whitechurch, Rathfarnham, Co. Dublin. Her grave, which she shares with a relative, is marked by an attractive headstone.

Esmé Stuart 'Lennox' Robinson (1886–1958), who is buried in

78. *St Paul's churchyard, Ardmore, Co. Waterford.*

the close of St Patrick's Cathedral, worked in the Abbey Theatre for many years as a playwright, manager and director. Twenty of his plays were staged there, including *The whiteheaded boy* and *Drama at Inish*. He is commemorated in a stained glass window at St Multose's, Kinsale, Co. Cork.

Also buried in the close of St Patrick's Cathedral is the playwright Denis Johnston (1901–84) and his wife Betty Chancellor. A barrister

79.
*Commemorative
window to
Lennox Robinson
and Stewart and
Nora Dorman in
St Multose's,
Kinsale, Co.
Cork.*

I COME LORD TO BE WITH
THEE AND BLESS THEE

by profession, his first controversial play, *The old lady says no*, was
rejected by the Abbey Theatre but was a great success when staged at
the Gate Theatre, where he later became director for a number of
years. Following other successes at the same venue, he left Dublin in
1935 to join the BBC, for whom he worked as a war correspondent.

80. St Patrick's Cathedral churchyard.

His experiences in the latter role are vividly described in his memoir *Nine rivers from Jordan*. Inscribed on his tombstone are the following lines from *The old lady says no*, referring to Dublin:

> 'Strumpet city in the sunset
> Wilful city of savage dreamers,
> So old, so sick with memories
> Old mother;
> Some they say are damned,
> But you, I know, will walk the streets of Paradise
> Head high, and unashamed.'

Another well-known war correspondent, Lionel Thomas Fleming (1904–74), is buried in the grounds of the Church of the Ascension, Timoleague, Co. Cork.

The artist Paul Henry (1876–1958), son of a Church of Ireland rector, is particularly associated with Achill Island, where he lived for seven years and produced some of the most powerful and evocative paintings of the landscape and people of the west of Ireland. Probably no artist working in that part of the country is better known, more popular or so easily recognisable. He is buried in St Patrick's churchyard, Enniskerry, Co. Wicklow, with his second wife Mabel, the grave being marked by a somewhat featureless lump of granite.

Mary Catherine (May) Guinness (1863–1955), who is interred in the churchyard at Whitechurch, Rathfarnham, Co. Dublin, was a less well-known artist who nevertheless exhibited widely and is included in many important collections. She lived and worked for long periods in France, where she studied under André Lhote, and was an important influence on many painters, including Mainie Jellett and Evie Hone. On the outbreak of the Great War, at the age of 52, she joined the French army as a military nurse and was awarded the Croix de Guerre.

Another son of the rectory, Sir Hugh Lane (1875–1915), the art dealer and collector, is commemorated by a tablet in St Ann's Church, Dawson Street, Dublin. He was the founder of the Municipal Gallery of Modern Art (the Hugh Lane Gallery) but is best known for his gift of 39 French paintings, which, following a contested will, are now shared between Dublin and the National Gallery, London, on a five-year rotation. He was drowned when the SS *Lusitania* was torpedoed by a German submarine in 1915.

Turlough O'Carolan (1670–1738), known as 'the last of the Irish bards', was blinded by smallpox at the age of eighteen, but with the help of Mrs MacDermott Roe of Alderford, Co. Roscommon, became an itinerant harper. He also composed and had his music published during his lifetime. Welcome in the 'Big Houses' of Ulster and Connacht, there is a fine marble memorial to him in St Patrick's Cathedral, erected 'by the desire of Sydney Lady Morgan' (sculptor: J. V. Hogan).

A simple marble plaque in St Malachi's Church, Hillsborough, Co. Down, remembers William Harty, who died in 1918 and was organist there for 40 years. His son was Sir Hamilton Harty (1879–1941,) musician, composer and famous conductor of the

ERECTED
BY THE DESIRE OF SYDNEY LADY MORGAN
TO THE MEMORY OF
CAROLAN
THE LAST OF THE IRISH BARDS

OBIIT
A·D·MDCCXXXVIII·AETATIS·SVAE·AN·LXVIII

81. Turlough O'Carolan in St Patrick's Cathedral.

Hallé Orchestra.

James Gandon (1742–1823) is Ireland's greatest neo-classical architect. His great works changed the face of Dublin and include the Four Courts, the Custom House and King's Inns. He was a great friend of the antiquarian and topographical draughtsman Francis Grose (1731–91) and expressed the wish to be buried with him. They rest together in Drumcondra churchyard, Dublin, under a large raised stone slab. Grose was a friend of the Scottish poet

82. St Malachi's, Hillsborough, Co. Down.

Robert Burns, who alluded to him in the lines:

'A chiel's among you taking notes,
and faith he'll prent it'.

Mrs Cecil Frances Alexander (1818–95) was a poet and writer who published a number of hymns which are amongst the most popular in the English-speaking world, including 'All things bright and beautiful', 'There is a green hill far away' and 'Once in royal David's city'. She is commemorated in a stained glass window in the baptistry of St Columb's Cathedral, Derry, where her husband, William, was bishop.

In the musicians' corner of Christ Church Cathedral is the incomplete memorial to Sir John Andrew Stevenson (1761–1833), who is best remembered for his accompaniments to Moore's Irish melodies. It includes a bust of the deceased and a single choirboy (sculptor: Thomas Kirk). There should have been two choirboys, but the second was withheld by the sculptor when the balance of his fees remained unpaid!

Alexander Irvine (1863–1941), the preacher, author and social philosopher, was born into a poverty-stricken family in Antrim. He joined the Royal Marines, where he learned to read. In 1888 he emigrated to New York, where he studied theology and worked amongst the destitute in the slums. He is mainly remembered as a novelist, however, his best-known work being *My lady of the chimney corner*. He died in California, but his ashes were brought back to

83. Grave of James Gandon and Captain Francis Grose at Drumcondra Church, Dublin.

84. Cecil Frances Alexander, poetess and hymn-writer (1818–95). (Photographer unknown)

Ireland and laid to rest with his parents, Anna and Jamie, in the graveyard of Antrim Parish Church. The spot is marked by a fine memorial stone paid for by an admirer.

Also buried in the same churchyard but in an unmarked grave is George Victor Du Noyer RHA (1817–69) and his four-year-old daughter, both of whom died of scarlet fever. Of Huguenot descent, Du Noyer was an eminent geologist whose field sheets are considered works of art. He was also a fine painter of marine life, plants and fungi whose works are in the archives of the Natural History Museum and the National Botanical Gardens, Dublin. There was an exhibition of his work in the National Gallery of Ireland in 1995.

Sir William Wilde (1815–76), the eminent ear and eye surgeon, prolific author and father of Oscar Wilde, had three illegitimate children, two of whom are buried in the graveyard at St Molua's, Drumsnatt, Co. Monaghan. A simple headstone reads:

'To the memory of two loving and beloved
sisters. Emily Wilde 24. Mary Wilde 22.'

They were preparing for a party on Hallowe'en night 1871 when one girl's ball gown caught fire; as her sister tried to put out the flames, the blaze spread to her dress too. Both died some days later.

The architect George Semple is buried close to the entrance to Drumcondra Church, Dublin. The inscription on the tombstone reads:

'Here lieth the body of Mr George Semple of the City
of Dublin, Architect, whose skill in his profession, simplicity of
manners,
unaffected piety, and rectitude of heart,
gained him the applause of all good men. He departed
this life on the 13th day of April, 1782, aged 73 years.
His daughter, Eliza Keatinge, ordered this stone and inscription to
be done as a small, but grateful mark of filial duty.'

He is chiefly remembered as the designer of Essex Bridge, Dublin, and the spire of St Patrick's Cathedral, but also as the uncle of John Semple Senior (1763–1840), who, with his son John Semple Junior (1801–82), designed some of the most remarkable Church of Ireland churches in the early nineteenth century.

9. SOLDIERS OF THE BRITISH EMPIRE

Countless soldiers from a Church of Ireland background served the British Empire loyally for three centuries, and military memorials abound. Many are of a heroic nature.

The death of Lieutenant Neville Josiah Aylmer Coghill, serving with the Warwickshire Regiment in South Africa, is commemorated by a plaque in Drumcondra Church, Dublin, and by stained glass in St Barrahane's Church, Castletownsend, Co. Cork. On 22 January 1879 he was part of a British force of 1,800 men who were attacked and wiped out by 20,000 Zulus at the Battle of Isandhlwana. As the battle neared its end, an effort was made to save the regimental colours, and this task was given to Coghill and another officer. While crossing a river in full flood with the Zulus in hot pursuit, the flag was swept away and they lost their horses but managed to swim to the other side. There, with their backs against a large boulder, they made their last stand. When their bodies were discovered, a ring of dead Zulus was found around them. Both were posthumously awarded the Victoria Cross. Also killed in the same battle was Lieutenant George Fredrick Hodson, commemorated by a fine mosaic plaque at Christ Church, Delgany, Co. Wicklow.

In July of the same year the British army again advanced into Zululand. Scouting ahead of the main force was a detachment of the 9th Lancers including Captain Lord William Leslie de la Poer Beresford, on leave from his job as aide-de-camp to the viceroy of India. While crossing a river they were attacked by a Zulu war party, and during the fighting a Sergeant Fitzmaurice fell to the ground when his horse stumbled. Beresford immediately went to his assistance and kept the enemy at bay with well-aimed pistol shots until Fitzmaurice could mount up behind him. Both men eventually reached safety and Beresford was awarded the Victoria Cross. His memorial is in Holy Trinity, Clonegam, Co. Waterford,

85. Major-General Henry Davis, who succeeded the duke of Wellington as commander of the Indian Army, in St Mary's, Newry, Co. Down.

the burial church of the Beresford family.

Captain Henry C. J. Lloyd was killed in 1879 at Islandula during the same campaign and is remembered by an impressive imperial memorial in Monaghan Parish Church. A relief in the centre shows two soldiers watching over his grave while, in the background, some Boers approach. At the side are two armed Zulu warriors, and at the base a reliquary containing a medal in pristine condition, showing Queen Victoria's head in profile.

Many soldiers served and died in the 'little wars' of the Empire. Lieutenant Robert Doran of the 18th Royal Irish Regiment fell at the storming of the Shoe Dagon Pagoda in Rangoon, Burma (now Myanmar), in 1852, at the age of 25. He is remembered in St Iberius's Church, Wexford, and in the 1852–3 Burma War

86. *Detail from the memorial window to Lieutenant Neville J. A. Coghill VC in St Barrahane's, Castletownsend, Co. Cork.*

87. *Detail from the memorial to Captain Henry C. J. Lloyd in St Patrick's, Monaghan.*

DEATH OF LIEUT COL. TOMLINSON
Com⁹ 18ᵀ (Royal Irish) Reg.
AT CHAPPOO 18ᵀᴴ MAY 1842

IN MEMORY OF
JAMES GALBRAITH
LIEUT. COLONEL COMMANDING THE 66ᵀᴴ ROYAL BERKSHIRE REGIMENT
SON OF SAMUEL GALBRAITH. CLANABOGAN.
KILLED IN ACTION JULY 27ᵀᴴ 1880, AT MAIWAND, WHERE HIS BODY RESTS.

Memorial in St Patrick's Cathedral, Dublin.

Another soldier of the same regiment, Lieutenant Colonel R. Tomlinson, was killed at the Battle of Chappoo in China in May 1842. There is a bas-relief, also in St Patrick's Cathedral, showing two soldiers tending him as he lies wounded on the ground while others stand around. It forms part of the monument (sculptor: Terence Farrell) to the memory of all soldiers of the regiment who fell during the China War of 1840–2.

When the British ruled India, war was endemic in the Punjab and the north-west frontier region, as the tribes were in an almost constant state of revolt. A memorial in Derry Cathedral recounts how Captain John Owen Lucas of the 29th Regiment died at the Battle of Ferozeshah in 1845 'whilst in the act of cheering on his men'. Captain Charles E. MacDonnell of the same regiment also fought at Ferozeshah and was subsequently severely wounded at the Battle of Sobraon. He died, aged 29, when 'his health sank from the effect of his wound and continued active service under the sun of India'. His memorial is in Monkstown Parish Church. Captain Henry Needham, another officer severely wounded at the Battle of Sobraon, survived and returned to County Kerry, where he died 40 years later. He is remembered by a wall-tablet in the church of St Michael and All Angels, Waterville.

Lieutenant Colonel James Galbraith, commanding the 66th Royal Berkshire Regiment, died in action at the Battle of Maiwand during the Afghan war of 1878–80 and is commemorated by a fine sculpture in Clanabogan Parish Church, Co. Tyrone. This shows him holding the regimental flag and pointing his sword at the enemy as he falls mortally wounded (sculptor: Sir Thomas Brock). Lieutenant Richard Trevor Chute of the 66th Regiment also died in this battle, aged 23, and his memorial tablet is in Ballymacelligott Church, near Tralee, Co. Kerry.

The British lost the Battle of Maiwand. As they retreated, assailed on all sides by the local tribesmen, Lieutenant Thomas Rice Henn of the Royal Engineers with ten men acted as a rearguard that stemmed the enemy advance and helped many of their comrades to escape. None of the rearguard survived. Field

88 (top left). St Patrick's Cathedral: Lieutenant Colonel Tomlinson dies at the Battle of Chappoo, China.

89 (left). Galbraith memorial, Clanabogan Parish Church, Co. Tyrone.

90. Detail from the memorial to Lieutenant Charles Westenra in St Patrick's, Monaghan (sculptor: Thomas Kirk).

Marshall Sir Garnet Wolseley said of Henn: 'No hero ever died more nobly than he did—I envy the manner of his death—if I had ten sons, I should be indeed proud if all ten fell as he fell'. Henn's memorial is in St Patrick's Cathedral.

Sir Bindon Blood (1842–1940), to whom there is a memorial in St Columba's Church, Ennis, Co. Clare, was a celebrated general on the north-west frontier. The young cavalry officer Winston Churchill was under his command during a revolt of the Pathan tribesmen in 1896 and described him as 'a striking figure in those savage mountains and among those wild, rifle-armed clansmen'. He was a direct descendant of the notorious Colonel Blood who attempted to steal the crown jewels in the reign of King Charles II, and considered this event the most glorious in the family history.

There is a tablet in Donadea Church, Co. Kildare, in memory of Lieutenant General Sir Fenton Aylmer, who also served on the north-west frontier and won the Victoria Cross as a Royal Engineers officer in the Hunza Campaign of 1891. The culmination of the operation was the capture of an important fort, during which Aylmer, under heavy fire, placed a guncotton charge against the main gate and was shot in the leg as he lit the fuse. He retreated to await the explosion, but when the guncotton failed to explode he went forward again to relight the fuse. He was severely injured by a rock thrown from the fort, but the charge exploded and the fort was taken. Despite his injuries, he took part in the fighting and killed several of the enemy before fainting through loss of blood. He died in 1935, aged 73.

THE NAPOLEONIC WARS (1792–1815)

The greatest conflict of the eighteenth and nineteenth centuries was the war against Napoleon. Until the final campaign, the British army, commanded by the duke of Wellington, fought mainly in Spain and Portugal in what came to be known as the Peninsular War (1804–14). It is estimated that at least 100,000 Irish soldiers and sailors served in the army and Royal Navy during the Napoleonic Wars, and that 30,000 of these were recruited in 1793 and 1794.

Colonel Sir William Cox (1777–1864) is commemorated in Monkstown Parish Church, Co. Dublin. In August 1810 he was in command of the garrison at the town of Almeida in Portugal, an important fortress on the frontier with Spain, under siege by the French. This was the last obstacle they faced before Lisbon, but the duke of Wellington was hopeful that it would hold out for two months. Owing to a freak accident, however, the main gunpowder and ammunition magazine exploded, killing 500 soldiers instantly, and a few days later the British were forced to surrender. Their regular troops were sent to France as prisoners, but Cox was offered and accepted parole on condition that he did not serve in

TO THE MEMORY OF

COLONEL

OHN TOWNSEND,

LATE OF THE 14TH LIGHT DRAGOONS.

HE SERVED WITH DISTINCTION

IN PORTUGAL, SPAIN, AND FRANCE.

HE DIED ON THE 22TH OF APRIL,

1845.

THIS MONUMENT

IS ERECTED

BY HIS BROTHER OFFICERS.

91. Colonel John Townsend memorial at St Barrahane's, Castletownsend, Co. Cork.

the war again. He died in 1864, aged 87.

Nearly two years later, on 6 April 1812, the British lost 3,500 men, the flower of the army, during the final assault on the city of Badajoz in Spain, which had been under siege for three weeks and was fiercely defended. Among those who died was Captain Henry Tenison Bellingham, who 'fell gallantly leading his men', as described in the tablet to his memory in St Mary's Church, Castlebellingham, Co. Louth. He was 26. Lieutenant Colonel John Browne fought throughout the war and was wounded at Badajoz. He recovered to fight at Waterloo, where he was wounded three more times and left for dead on the battlefield. When they came to bury him 48 hours later, however, he was still alive and made such a good recovery that he lived for another 34 years. His memorial is in Christ Church, Castlebar, Co. Mayo.

Another Peninsular War veteran, Colonel John Townsend, is remembered by an attractive military monument in St Barrahane's Church, Castletownsend, Co. Cork. It was erected by his brother officers and displays a soldier's greatcoat, shako, sword and pistol. He died in 1845.

Colonel Edward W. Drewe (1782–1862) also served in the Peninsula and is commemorated by a military memorial in Monkstown Parish Church. As a 33-year-old lieutenant in the Royal Inniskilling Fusiliers he later fought at Waterloo, where he was severely wounded when the regiment resisted French cavalry charges in the early stages of the battle. The monument depicts his helmet, sword and Waterloo medal, the first to be awarded to all soldiers regardless of rank. On retirement from the army he lived in Kingstown (Dún Laoghaire) and was a regular churchgoer at Monkstown. He died in 1862 at the age of 80.

92. Detail of memorial to Colonel Edward Ward Drewe in Monkstown, Co. Dublin, including his sword, shako and Waterloo medal.

In 1814 Napoleon's empire was crumbling, and as he retreated to France he left behind isolated garrisons that had to be subjugated. Bergen-op-Zoom, north of Antwerp, was one such, and it was there that Brigadier Arthur Gore died as he led his regiment in the assault on the town. There is an elaborate memorial to him in St George's Church, Goresbridge, Co. Kilkenny, which incorporates a sarcophagus with a relief showing the storming of the ramparts (sculptor: John Smyth).

Amongst those buried in the simple granite Gough family vault in the churchyard of St Brigid's Church, Stillorgan, Co. Dublin, is the Limerick-born Field Marshal Sir Hugh Gough (1779–1869). Commissioned at the age of fourteen, he fought in the Peninsular War and was knighted for bravery by King Ferdinand VII of Spain. In 1841 he was commander of the army in China, where his victories helped to bring about the cession of Hong Kong to the British government. He ended his career as field marshal and commander-in-chief of the Indian Army and returned to Ireland in 1851, where he lived at St Helen's House, Booterstown, Co. Dublin (now the Radisson Hotel). In 1878 a magnificent equestrian statue, the work of John Henry Foley, was erected in his memory on the main avenue of the Phoenix Park, where it remained until blown up by the IRA in the 1950s. Sir Winston Churchill (1874–1965) believed that his first coherent memory was the unveiling of this statue by the viceroy, his grandfather.

A military memorial with cannon, flags and drums in the chancel of St Multose's Church, Kinsale, Co. Cork, remembers Lt. Gen. Sir Thomas Reynell (1777–1848), who fought in the Peninsular War and was wounded at Waterloo. This did not prevent him from entering Paris three weeks later, where he participated in the Allied victory parade at the head of the Light Brigade!

Major Arthur R. Heyeand survived the Peninsular War but died at Waterloo and was buried at Mont St Jean, close to the battlefield. His marble memorial in St Patrick's Church, Coleraine, Co. Londonderry, describes how he fell, leading the 40th Regiment of foot, in the moment of victory. The final words of his epitaph read 'He knew his duty and he did it'.

On the left-hand side of the choir in St Macartin's Cathedral, Enniskillen, Co. Fermanagh, is a life-size statue of General Sir Galbraith Lowry Cole of the Inniskilling Fusiliers, who commanded the 4th Division during the Peninsular War and was present at the decisive battles of Vittoria, Salamanca and Toulouse.

93. *Major-General George O'Malley in the churchyard at Christ Church, Castlebar, Co. Mayo.*

He is also commemorated by a statue on a column in the town's public park (both sculpted by Terence Farrell).

A memorial to Major General Sir Denis Pack in Kilkenny Cathedral includes a bust of the deceased and a depiction of his Peninsular Cross with clasps and Waterloo medal (sculptor: Sir Francis Chantrey). He played an important role in the battles of Salamanca and Toulouse, and commanded the Scottish Highland Regiments at Waterloo.

Major General George O'Malley (1780–1847), whose somewhat dilapidated statue stands alongside Christ Church, Castlebar, Co. Mayo, served in North America, the West Indies, Egypt and the Mediterranean. He also commanded the 2nd Battalion, 44th

Regiment, at Waterloo, where he was twice wounded. He subsequently became commander of the 88th Regiment, later to achieve fame as the Connaught Rangers.

Captain Alexander Walker of the 38th Regiment has a memorial in Castlepollard Parish Church, Co. Westmeath, erected by his brother officers. This remarkable soldier saw action in many of the major battles of the Peninsular War and, 40 years later, fought in the Crimean War and the Indian Mutiny. He died of cholera in the East Indies in 1867.

Included in a memorial to the Kingsmill family in the deconsecrated church of St Mary's in Kilkenny city is William Kingsmill (born 1793), who served in the 6th Regiment and was a

94. St Mary's Cathedral, Limerick.

member of the garrison guarding Napoleon during his imprisonment on St Helena.

THE CRIMEAN WAR (1853–6)

The next great war involving the European powers was between Russia on the one side and Britain and France (now allies), the Ottoman (Turkish) Empire and, later, Sardinia-Piedmont on the other. The main battleground was the Crimean peninsula in south-ern Russia, where well over half a million men died, mainly from disease, hunger and cold. Although the number of British soldiers was much less than those from France and Turkey, over 22,000 died. The Allies were victorious following the siege and capture of the port of Sebastopol, but only after famous and bloody battles at Alma, Balaklava and Inkerman. Lieutenant Henry George Donovan was present at all of these battles and died on 8 September 1855, the day that Sebastopol finally fell. According to his memorial tablet in Ferns Cathedral, Co. Wexford, he was interred in the family burial-ground at Ballymore a year later, and it would be interesting to know how his body came back to Ireland—perhaps, like Admiral Nelson after his death at Trafalgar, in a brandy barrel!

Lieutenant Thomas Kidd also died at Sebastopol, and a relief on his memorial in Armagh Cathedral shows a dying soldier being supported by one of his comrades (sculptor: Sir Thomas Farrell). Another to die in the early days of the siege was Captain Bingham Muller of the Royal Regiment, who is buried in a soldiers' grave on Cathcart's Hill on the shores of the Crimea. He is remembered by a military memorial in St Mary's Cathedral, Limerick. Also present was Captain Richard Eyre, remembered by a marble memorial in St John the Baptist's Church, Eyrecourt, Co. Galway. He survived the war but died eleven years later at Blackrock, Co. Dublin, aged 33. Also buried at Cathcart's Hill is Colonel Henry Clermont Cobbe (1811–55) of the 4th 'King's Own' Regiment, who died of wounds in June 1855 while leading the left wing of the army in one of many unsuccessful attempts to capture the city during the eleven-month siege.

In St Peter's churchyard, Drogheda, Co. Louth, is the interesting tombstone, engraved with his regimental badge, of John Duggan, who fought throughout the war as a private in the

111

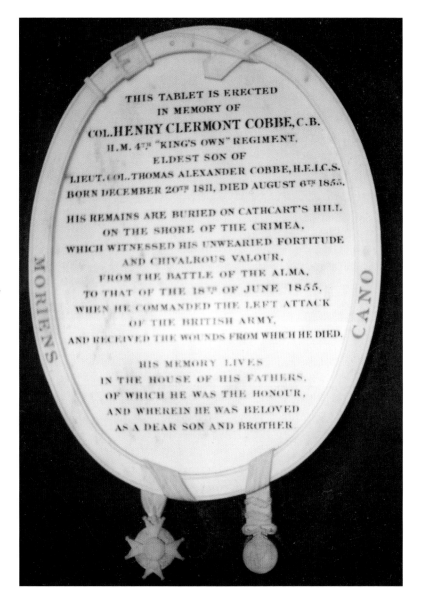

MORIENS CANO

THIS TABLET IS ERECTED
IN MEMORY OF
COL. HENRY CLERMONT COBBE, C.B.
H.M. 4TH "KING'S OWN" REGIMENT,
ELDEST SON OF
LIEUT. COL. THOMAS ALEXANDER COBBE, H.E.I.C.S.
BORN DECEMBER 20TH 1811, DIED AUGUST 6TH 1855.

HIS REMAINS ARE BURIED ON CATHCART'S HILL
ON THE SHORE OF THE CRIMEA,
WHICH WITNESSED HIS UNWEARIED FORTITUDE
AND CHIVALROUS VALOUR,
FROM THE BATTLE OF THE ALMA,
TO THAT OF THE 18TH OF JUNE 1855,
WHEN HE COMMANDED THE LEFT ATTACK
OF THE BRITISH ARMY,
AND RECEIVED THE WOUNDS FROM WHICH HE DIED.

HIS MEMORY LIVES
IN THE HOUSE OF HIS FATHERS,
OF WHICH HE WAS THE HONOUR,
AND WHEREIN HE WAS BELOVED
AS A DEAR SON AND BROTHER.

95. St Patrick's, Donabate, Co. Dublin.

17th Lancers. On his retirement from the army he became sexton of St Peter's and remained in Drogheda until his death in 1881, aged 67.

Major General William Mussenden of the 8th King's Royal Irish Hussars is remembered by a marble plaque in St Patrick's Cathedral. As an eighteen-year-old cornet of horse he took part in the famous charge of the Light Brigade at Balaclava and was also present at the other principal battles of the war. He later served in the Indian Mutiny and died in 1910, aged 74. The memorial was

SACRED
TO THE MEMORY OF
JOHN DUGGAN
WHO DIED IN DROCHEDA MARCH 22, 1881
AGED 67 YEARS.

LATE PRIVATE 17 LANCERS
AND SEXTON OF ST PETER'S CHURCH
HE FOUGHT IN THE BATTLES OF
ALMA INKERMAN. SEVASTOPOL. AND
BALAKLAVA.

"I KNOW WHOM I HAVE BELIEVED"
2. TIMOTHY 1. 12.
"I HAVE FOUGHT A GOOD FIGHT
I HAVE FINISHED MY COURSE
I HAVE KEPT THE FAITH"
2. TIMOTHY 4. 7.

96. St Peter's churchyard, Drogheda, Co. Louth.

raised by officers of the regiment.

Captain Charles Thomas King, orderly officer to Lord Raglan, the British commander-in-chief, was also at Balaclava, where he died of cholera, a disease that claimed the lives of thousands of soldiers throughout the war. He is remembered by a memorial in St Stephen's Church, Upper Mount Street, Dublin, as is Captain Jackson Wray of the Connaught Rangers, who was also killed during the siege.

Lieutenant Colonel William Hoey (1815–54) commanded the 30th Regiment at the victorious Battle of Alma, which allowed the allies to advance on Sebastopol. Despite heavy casualties he escaped uninjured, only to succumb to cholera five days later. His fine wall monument is in Monkstown Parish Church, Co. Dublin.

THE INDIAN MUTINY (1857–9)

The Indian Mutiny broke out the year after the Crimean War ended and required almost as great a military effort to suppress. It was caused by the revolt of thousands of sepoys (Indian soldiers in the service of the East India Company) and began with the massacre of Europeans at Meerut in May 1857. During most of the previous 100 years the sepoys had been loyal to their British masters, but for a variety of reasons, including government reforms that threatened their way of life, they became uneasy and feared for the future. Matters came to a head when it was rumoured that the grease used in the cartridges supplied with the new Enfield rifles consisted of a mixture of cow and pig fat, both considered unclean by Hindus and Moslems alike. After Meerut the mutiny spread to other parts of India, with the main uprising in the north, where Delhi was soon captured and Lucknow besieged.

The recapture of Delhi was essential for the reassertion of British power, and after a long and difficult siege it was successfully stormed on 14 September 1857. There is a fine work by the celebrated sculptor John Henry Foley in Lisburn Cathedral, Co. Antrim, in memory of Brigadier General John Nicholson (1821–57), who was mortally wounded on that day while leading the assault. Nicholson, the eldest of five sons of an Irish doctor, was an inspiring commander of superb physique and a messianic frame of mind, who during the mutiny dealt with his enemies ruthlessly. Earlier, as an administrator in the Punjab he had stamped out lawlessness with the utmost severity, pursuing criminals personally and displaying their severed heads upon his desk. His strange and forceful personality so impressed the natives that some worshipped him as their spiritual guide and deity, falling down at his feet in reverent submission. The latter was an offence punishable by 36 strokes of the cat-o'-nine-tails, but even this failed to deter their devotion. Major George Ogle Jacob, commanding the Bengal European Fusiliers, also died in Delhi on the same day.

IN MEMORY OF
GEORGE OCLE JACOB
MAJOR I⁹ᵗ BENGAL EUROPEAN FUSILIERS,
WHO WHILST COMMANDING HIS REGIMENT
FELL MORTALLY WOUNDED AT THE STORMING OF DELHI
ON THE 14ᵀᴴ SEPTEMBER 1857 AND DIED THE SAME DAY,
AGED 38 YEARS AND SIX MONTHS.

"THEM ALSO WHICH SLEEP IN JESUS
WILL GOD BRING WITH HIM."
I.THES. 4. 14.

97. St Iberius's, Wexford.

His memorial is in St Iberius's Church, Wexford. Captain Francis Spring, of the 24th Regiment, died two months previously in another encounter with mutineers and is commemorated in St John's Church, Tralee, Co. Kerry.

Queen Victoria (1819–1901) inaugurated the Victoria Cross in 1856, and this medal, made from melted-down Russian cannon captured at Sebastopol, is only awarded for acts of conspicuous bravery on the battlefield. A remarkable number of Irishmen involved in the Mutiny were recipients, including Assistant Surgeon William Bradshaw VC, who was decorated for saving the lives of wounded soldiers in Lucknow despite the close proximity of mutineers and although injured himself. He is commemorated by a Good Samaritan motif in St Mary's Church, Thurles, Co. Tipperary (sculptor: J. R. Kirk). Assistant Surgeon Valentine M. McMaster VC was in Lucknow at the same time as Bradshaw and received his medal for constantly exposing himself to heavy fire, during which he brought to safety and tended many wounded. He is remembered on a memorial in St Columb's Cathedral, Derry.

*98. Monkstown
Parish Church,
Co. Dublin.*

Sergeant-Major George Lambert VC received his decoration for demonstrating great courage on three separate occasions, the last of which was at Lucknow. There is a memorial to him in Mullabrack Church, Co. Armagh.

Lieutenant General John C. Guise VC, who also served in the Crimea, acted most gallantly throughout the relief of Lucknow, during which he saved the life of a fellow officer before going out under heavy fire to help two other wounded men. There is an attractive brass plaque to his memory in Christ Church, Gorey, Co. Wexford, erected by Gorey YMCA and members of his Sunday school class.

IN MEMORY OF
CAPTAIN HENRY MAXWELL HOWARD,
18ᵀᴴ HUSSARS,
WHO DIED AT MADRAS FEBᵞ 11ᵀᴴ 1875,
AGED 38 YEARS.

ERECTED BY HIS BROTHER OFFICERS.

99. Killiskey, Co. Wicklow (sculptor: T. H. Hartley).

Lieutenant Colonel Thomas B. Hackett VC was a lieutenant in the Royal Welsh Fusiliers at the second relief of Lucknow when he led a rescue party that saved a wounded fellow officer from certain death. Later the same day and under fire he climbed onto the roof of a bungalow his men were defending and cut away the thatch to prevent its being set alight by mutineers. There is a memorial to him in the Marshall family vault in Lockeen churchyard, Co. Tipperary, and in the east window of Lockeen Church.

These five recipients of Britain's highest military honour were lucky to survive, but many other Irishmen at Lucknow were not so fortunate. Lieutenant John Wall of the Royal Irish Fusiliers was killed there on 14 March 1858. Nine days later in the same area Frederick J. MacDonnell, second in command of the 2nd Punjab Cavalry, died in action, aged 25. His father, the Reverend Richard MacDonnell, was Provost of Trinity College, Dublin. Both soldiers are commemorated by fine memorials in Monkstown Church, Co. Dublin.

With Delhi and Lucknow secure, it was only a matter of time before the mutiny was finally crushed. There was still a lot of fighting, however, and in 1858 Lieutenant General Harry H. Lyster VC (then a lieutenant in the Bengal Native Infantry) received his decoration 'for gallantly charging and breaking singly, a skirmishing square of the retreating rebel army and killing a number of sepoys in the process'. He died in 1922, aged 92, and there is a tablet to his memory in St Brigid's Church, Stillorgan, Co. Dublin. His nephew, Major General Hamilton L. Reed, also won the Victoria Cross.

A headstone in the churchyard of St John's Church, Longford, with a facsimile of the Victoria Cross inscribed, marks the last resting-place of Private Joseph Ward VC. He fought throughout the Crimean War and the Mutiny but was decorated for his part in the charge of the 8th King's Royal Irish Hussars at Gwalior in 1858, when the rebels were routed and two guns captured. The headstone was raised by the officers and men of his troop and includes the following lines:

'Soldier rest thy warfare o'er
Sleep the sleep that knows no breaking
Dream of battlefields no more
Morn of sorrow night of waking'.

Lieutenant General Sir Henry M. Havelock-Allan VC was a 27-year-old lieutenant (and aide-de-camp to his father) when at Cawnpore in 1857, under a shower of shot and grape, he charged and dispersed a party of mutineers and captured their last 24-pounder gun. Later, at Lucknow, he again demonstrated extraordinary courage and was recommended for, but did not receive, a second Victoria Cross. The quintessential imperial army officer of the nineteenth century, he also served in Persia and in the Maori

Wars (1863–6). He died in 1897, probably as he would have wished, shot by tribesmen while riding ahead of his escort in the Khyber Pass during the North-West Frontier War (1897–8). His brass monument in St Patrick's Cathedral was erected by the officers and men of the Royal Irish Regiment, of which he was colonel.

The Indian Mutiny was a disaster for all concerned, with appalling acts of savagery committed by both sides. When it ended in 1859 the native army was radically reformed and, largely owing to Lord Canning (1812–62) and his supporters, a spirit of reconciliation was encouraged. Thereafter the British ruled India for a further 90 years, and for most of that time, including two world wars, the native soldiers of the Indian army served the British Empire loyally and bravely.

THE BOER WAR (1899–1902)

When the Boers (Afrikaners) of South Africa declared war on the British in 1899, it was felt that they had little hope of success against the might of the Empire and would be defeated by Christmas. In fact, it proved to be the longest, the costliest, the bloodiest and the most humiliating war that Britain fought between 1815 and 1914. It gave the British, as Rudyard Kipling said, 'no end of a lesson'. Irish regiments, including the Royal Dublin Fusiliers, the Royal Munster Fusiliers and the Connaught Rangers, were involved in the major battles and suffered heavy casualties. There are five Boer War memorials in St Patrick's Cathedral, one of which recalls the 83 men of the Royal Irish Lancers who made the supreme sacrifice. Top of the list is Colonel John S. Chisholme, who fell in one of the earliest battles, leading his dismounted men while waving a regimental scarf tied to a walking-stick.

The Battle of Spion Kop was fought on 24 January 1900 to capture a strategically important hill near Ladysmith then under siege by the Boers. After day-long heavy fighting, which cost 1,500 British casualties, the objective was taken, only to be abandoned the following day owing to inept leadership. A tablet in St Canice's Cathedral, Kilkenny, remembers Robert G. B. Riddell, commander of the 3rd Battalion King's Royal Rifles, who died leading his men during the assault.

*100. St Mary's
Cathedral,
Limerick.*

IN LOVING MEMORY OF
WILLIAM CROKER
MAJOR 27TH INNISKILLINGS
WHO DIED 21ST NOVBR 1887
AGED 62 YEARS
ALSO OF HIS ONLY SON
WILLIAM CHARLES ROBERT CROKER
2ND LIEUT 1ST ROYAL MUNSTER FUSILIERS
WHO REFUSING TO SURRENDER WAS
KILLED IN ACTION NEAR BOSHOF
SOUTH AFRICA ON 23RD FEBY 1902
AGED 19 YEARS
FAITHFUL UNTO DEATH

Private Robert Scott VC, who is buried in the graveyard of Christ Church, Kilkeel, Co. Down, won his Victoria Cross in 1900 at about the same time and in the same area. While defending a position on the outskirts of Ladysmith, and following heavy casualties, he and two other soldiers found themselves the only survivors. Despite being under continuous attack from a strong Boer force they held their post for fifteen hours without food and water until reinforcements arrived. Although wounded in the action, Scott soon returned to duty and continued to serve during the next four months of the siege without once being absent from duty. During the Great War he served as quartermaster sergeant with the Manchester Regiment, and when discharged joined the

Ulster Special Constabulary. When the Second World War broke out he was 65, but lied about his age and was accepted by the Royal Air Force, with whom he served until D-Day in 1944—truly a remarkable military career.

As the war progressed without any end in sight, more troops were needed and companies of mounted yeomanry were recruited from the aristocracy and landed gentry at home and in the colonies. Edward E. Wilmot-Chetwode served in the 45th (Dublin) Company of the Imperial Yeomanry and was wounded at Lindley, near Johannesburg, on 31 May 1900. This action involved the 13th (mainly Irish) Battalion of the yeomanry, which was forced to surrender after suffering severe casualties. The dead included the whiskey baronet Sir John Power. Lord Longford was severely wounded, and amongst the 500 taken prisoner were the earl of Leitrim and Lord Craigavon. Wilmot-Chetwode died of his wounds six weeks later, and his memorial is in St John's Church, Coolbanagher, Co. Laois. His name also appears on the brass memorial to the Imperial Yeomanry in St Patrick's Cathedral, as does that of Herbert J. Robinson, who was mortally wounded in the same engagement. He is remembered by a fine stained glass window in Christ Church, Delgany, Co. Wicklow. Three days later, in the same area, Second Lieutenant Ian F. Pollok of the 9th Lancers died from wounds received in action against Boers in full retreat from Johannesburg and Pretoria. At this stage the war appeared to have been won, but the enemy rallied and, using guerrilla tactics, held out for another two years. Pollok's memorial in the church of St John the Baptist, Eyrecourt, Co. Galway, includes the words:

'He gave his heart to his home,
His life for his country and his soul to his God'.

Colonel Eustace Guinness died at Bakenlaagte in October 1901 while commanding the 84th Battery, Royal Field Artillery. Under constant attack and with only three of his 32 gunners uninjured, he was trying to fire a round of case-shot when he was mortally wounded. He is remembered by a brass plate in St Brigid's, Stillorgan, Co. Dublin.

On 23 February 1902, nineteen-year-old Second Lieutenant William C. R. Croker of the Royal Munster Fusiliers was killed when he refused to surrender; his memorial, which also

*101. St
Nicholas's,
Eyrecourt, Co.
Galway.*

In Loving Memory of
IAN FREDERICK POLLOK,
2ND LIEUT. 9TH LANCERS.
3RD SON OF THE LATE JOHN POLLOK, D.L. LISMANY, BALLINASLOE.
WHO DIED 3RD JUNE 1900.
AT BOKSBURG, TRANSVAAL, FROM WOUNDS RECEIVED
IN ACTION 2ND JUNE AT BAPSFONTEIN.

HE GAVE HIS HEART TO HIS HOME
HIS LIFE FOR HIS COUNTRY, AND HIS SOUL TO HIS GOD.
"HE GIVETH HIS BELOVED SLEEP."
ERECTED BY HIS DEVOTED MOTHER, BROTHERS & SISTERS.

commemorates his father, Major William Croker of the 27th Inniskillings, is in St Mary's Cathedral, Limerick. Three months later the war ended with the Treaty of Vereeniging and the annexation of the Transvaal and the Orange Free State.

In that year the British Empire, on which the sun never set, covered roughly a quarter of the earth's land mass. A hundred years later it has ceased to exist, except for a few scattered outposts. *Sic transit gloria mundi.*

10. THE REBELLIONS OF 1798 AND 1803

The 1798 rebellion brought to an end what had been, by and large, a peaceful and progressive century. Encouraged by the success of the French and American revolutions, disparate elements in the country came together in the Society of the United Irishmen to seek a free and independent island by force of arms. When French help did not arrive until too late, the insurrection had little hope of success, and by the time it was suppressed over 35,000 people had died. Three of the leading rebel commanders, Wolfe Tone, Lord Edward Fitzgerald and Bagenal Harvey, were members of the Church of Ireland and all met violent deaths.

Captain Henry Cookes, a fencible (or yeoman soldier) who was killed at Kilcullen Bridge in May 1798, is commemorated by a military-style monument in St Patrick's, Carnalway, Co. Kildare (sculptor: Charles Regnart). Three other fencibles, Captain W. Chetwynd, Lieutenant W. H. Unite and Ensign J. Sparks, who were killed near Saintfield, are remembered in St Mary's, Comber, Co. Down. An inscribed stone on the wall beside the entrance to Christ Church, Castlebar, Co. Mayo, remembers five fencibles from the Frazer Highlanders who were killed trying to defend the church during the battle popularly known as 'the Races of Castlebar'.

Matthew Furlong, who was aide-de-camp to Bagenal Harvey, commander-in-chief of the Wexford rebel army, is buried in the graveyard of Killurin Church, Co. Wexford. He was shot dead while carrying a flag of truce prior to the commencement of the Battle of Ross on 5 June 1798, and there is a memorial to him and his comrades, Ann Flood and Thomas Cogley, on the avenue leading to the church.

A memorial in the churchyard at St Mary's, Castlecomer, Co. Kilkenny, remembers Martin Kearns, who was killed at the Battle of Castlecomer on 24 June 1798. It also records that his brother Páidin Rua was wounded in the same battle, and that another brother, Father Mogue Kearns, was executed for his part in the rising.

A stone beside the entrance to St Kevin's, Hollywood, Co. Wicklow, commemorates three rebels—Christopher Byrne, William Burke and Oliver Hoyle—who were killed on 27 January 1801 and buried in the churchyard.

James O'Connor was a rebel who fell at the Battle of Ballinamuck, and his name appears on the family tombstone close by Rathcline Church, Lanesborough, Co. Longford. To hide his involvement, the family dated his death to 25 August 1798, two weeks before the battle was fought!

The leaders of the United Irishmen were motivated by high ideals and the desire to create an independent Ireland to which Protestants, Catholics and Dissenters could give their allegiance. But when the rebellion broke out it degenerated into sectarianism in parts of the south, and both sides were responsible for atrocities on a horrific scale. The memorial in the graveyard of St Mary's, Old Ross, Co. Wexford, remembers the massacre of Protestants at Scullabogue and bears the following inscription:

'In Memoriam
In this place the people of Wexford
remember the victims of Scullabogue barn
interred here and at Templeshelin.
Used to detain some one hundred
men, women and children
the barn was set on fire on 5 June 1798,
the day of the Battle of Ross.
The remorse of the United Irish
at this outrage, a tragic departure
from their ideals, is shared
by the people of Ireland.'

Archibald Hamilton Rowan (1751–1834) was a wealthy landlord in County Down with close connections to the leading ruling families; he was also a Unitarian, a political radical and a United Irishman who was secretary of its Dublin Society in 1793. In that year Rowan, with a few companions, marched in green uniform with side-arms in a banned National Volunteers parade, after which he was accused of sedition, found guilty, fined £500 and sentenced to two years' imprisonment. He escaped to revolutionary France, where he was arrested as an English spy! After a period in prison in Brest,

In Memoriam

IN THIS PLACE THE PEOPLE OF WEXFORD
REMEMBER THE VICTIMS OF SCULLABOGUE BARN
INTERRED HERE AND AT TEMPLESHELIN.
USED TO DETAIN SOME ONE HUNDRED
MEN, WOMEN AND CHILDREN,
THE BARN WAS SET ON FIRE ON 5 JUNE 1798,
THE DAY OF THE BATTLE OF ROSS.
THE REMORSE OF THE UNITED IRISH
AT THIS OUTRAGE, A TRAGIC DEPARTURE
FROM THEIR IDEALS IS SHARED
BY THE PEOPLE OF IRELAND.

IN IOTLAINN DÉ GO DTUGTAR SINN

102. St Mary's churchyard, Old Ross, Co. Wexford.

he eventually proved his credentials and was brought to Paris, where he met Robespierre. He was disillusioned by the violence he saw there, including the death by guillotine of 60 people in a period of less than an hour and a half. After many adventures he sailed to the United States, where he found the life distasteful. His wife urged him to give up politics, and he eventually secured a pardon that allowed him to return home in 1804. He spent the last 30 years of his life in Killyleagh, Co. Down, where he was a kind and liberal-minded landlord and where there is a Celtic memorial cross in his honour in the graveyard of the Church of St John the Evangelist. He is also remembered by a tablet with military trophies within the church (sculptor: J. Robinson and son). Rowan was a most interesting man and his autobiography makes

103. Over the grave of Archibald Hamilton Rowan at St John the Evangelist's, Killyleagh, Co. Down.

fascinating reading.

The 1803 rebellion was a fiasco, and in retrospect seems more like a street riot than a serious attempt to create an Irish Republic. Confined to Dublin and involving less than 100 rebels, it was put down in a few days. Its Church of Ireland leaders, Robert Emmet

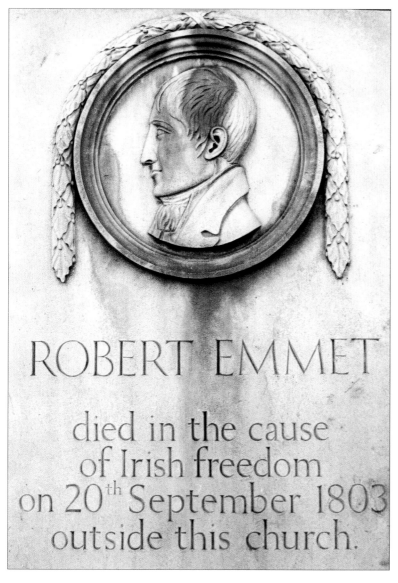

ROBERT EMMET

died in the cause
of Irish freedom
on 20th September 1803
outside this church.

104. Outside St Catherine's Church, Thomas Street, Dublin.

and Thomas Russell, were hanged. That would have been the end of the affair were it not for Emmet's famous speech from the dock, which made him an instant hero and probably did more to keep the flame of Irish nationalism alive than anything that happened in 1798. There is a plaque to his memory outside St Catherine's, Thomas Street, Dublin, the scene of his execution. A romantic aspect was his ill-fated love affair with Sarah Curran, a nationalist heroine, who died when she was 26. She was buried in an unmarked grave beside Newmarket Church (now deconsecrated), Co. Cork, where a headstone, recently restored, was raised many years later. Her father, the formidable lawyer and politician John Philpot Curran, completely disapproved of Emmet and refused to defend him at his trial. Curran is commemorated by a bust erected by public subscription in St Patrick's Cathedral (sculptor: Christopher Moore).

11. THE GREAT WAR (1914–18)

There is one memorial that is common to almost every church: that with the names of parishioners who served and died in the Great War, usually with its wreath of poppies left over from Remembrance Day. At that service the congregation would have heard the familiar and emotive words:

> 'They shall not grow old
> As we who are left grow old;
> Age shall not weary them
> Nor the years condemn.
> At the going down of the sun
> And in the morning
> We will remember them.'

Today it is difficult to imagine the extent of the casualties, but the number of dead on these Dublin memorials gives some idea of the loss suffered by so many families:

Holy Trinity, Rathmines	60
Christ Church, Leeson Park	48
St Stephen's, Mount Street	43
St John the Baptist, Clontarf	33
St Philip's and St James's, Booterstown	30
Monkstown Parish Church	28
Christ Church, Taney	20

The memorial at St Mary's, Crumlin Road, Belfast, records nearly 300 dead from that parish, most of whom fell on 1 July 1916, the opening day of the Battle of the Somme.

The standard communal memorial is a plaque of marble, stone or brass. For those who could afford it, however, stained glass was the choice and there are many beautiful examples. War memorial

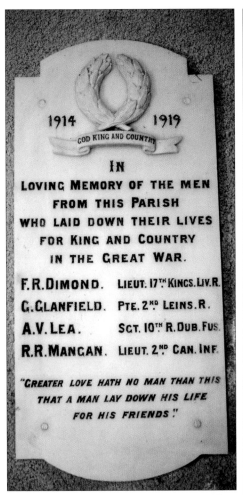

1914 1919

GOD KING AND COUNTRY

IN
LOVING MEMORY OF THE MEN
FROM THIS PARISH
WHO LAID DOWN THEIR LIVES
FOR KING AND COUNTRY
IN THE GREAT WAR.

F.R.DIMOND. LIEUT. 17TH KINGS.LIV.R.

G.GLANFIELD. PTE. 2ND LEINS.R.

A.V.LEA. SGT. 10TH R.DUB.FUS.

R.R.MANGAN. LIEUT. 2ND CAN.INF.

"GREATER LOVE HATH NO MAN THAN THIS
THAT A MAN LAY DOWN HIS LIFE
FOR HIS FRIENDS."

THIS TABLET IS ERECTED
TO THE GLORY OF GOD
AND IN HONOURED AND LOVING MEMORY OF
THOSE FROM THIS PARISH
WHO FELL IN THE GREAT WAR.
1914 — 1918.

SERGEANT JOHN Y. FOSTER.
CORP. WILLIE LEINSTER.
BOMBARDIER SAM FOSTER.
TROOPER HAL BEATTY.
PRIVATE CHARLES GILLILAND.
PRIVATE ROBERT HALLIDAY.
PRIVATE WILLIAM HAMILTON.
PRIVATE RICHARD HARRISON.
PRIVATE WILLIAM LEINSTER.
PRIVATE GEORGE PHAIR.
PRIVATE JOHN WALSH.
PRIVATE WILLIAM KERR.
"Greater love hath no man than this, that a man
lay down his life for his friends."

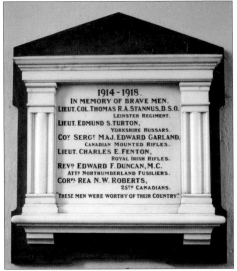

1914-1918.
IN MEMORY OF BRAVE MEN.
LIEUT. COL. THOMAS R.A. STANNUS, D.S.O.
LEINSTER REGIMENT.
LIEUT. EDMUND S. TURTON,
YORKSHIRE HUSSARS.
COY SERGT MAJ. EDWARD GARLAND,
CANADIAN MOUNTED RIFLES.
LIEUT. CHARLES E. FENTON,
ROYAL IRISH RIFLES.
REVD EDWARD F. DUNCAN, M.C.
ATTD NORTHUMBERLAND FUSILIERS.
CORPL REA N.W. ROBERTS,
25TH CANADIANS.
"THESE MEN WERE WORTHY OF THEIR COUNTRY."

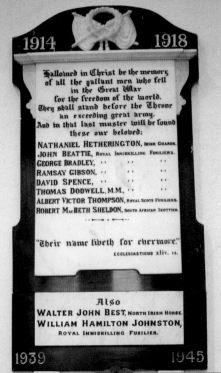

1914 1918

Hallowed in Christ be the memory
of all the gallant men who fell
in the Great War
for the freedom of the world.
They shall stand before the Throne
an exceeding great army.
And in that last muster will be found
these our beloved:

NATHANIEL HETHERINGTON, IRISH GUARDS.
JOHN BEATTIE, ROYAL INNISKILLING FUSILIERS.
GEORGE BRADLEY, '' '' ''
RAMSAY GIBSON, '' '' ''
DAVID SPENCE, '' '' ''
THOMAS DODWELL, M.M., '' '' ''
ALBERT VICTOR THOMPSON, ROYAL SCOTS FUSILIERS.
ROBERT MacBETH SHELDON, SOUTH AFRICAN SCOTTISH.

"Their name liveth for evermore."
ECCLESIASTICUS xliv. 14.

Also
WALTER JOHN BEST, NORTH IRISH HORSE.
WILLIAM HAMILTON JOHNSTON,
ROYAL INNISKILLING FUSILIER.

1939 1945

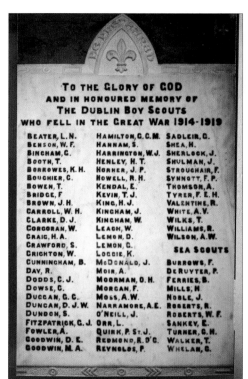

To the Glory of God
and in Honoured Memory of
The Dublin Boy Scouts
Who fell in the Great War 1914-1919

BEATER, L.N.	HAMILTON, G.C.M.	SADLEIR, G.
BENSON, W.F.	HANNAM, S.	SHEA, H.
BINGHAM, C.	HARRINGTON, W.J.	SHERLOCK, J.
BOOTH, T.	HENLEY, H.T.	SHULMAN, J.
BORROWES, K.H.	HORNER, J.P.	STROUGHAIR, F.
BOUCHIER, C.	HOWELL, R.H.	SYNNOTT, F.P.
BOWEN, T.	KENDAL, E.	THOMSON, A.
BRIDGE, F.	KEVIN, T.J.	TYRER, F.E.H.
BROWN, J.H.	KING, H.J.	VALENTINE, R.
CARROLL, W.H.	KINGHAM, J.	WHITE, A.V.
CLARKE, D.J.	KINGHAM, W.	WILKS, T.
CORCORAN, W.	LEACH, W.	WILLIAMS, R.
CRAIG, H.A.	LEMON, D.	WILSON, A.W.
CRAWFORD, S.	LEMON, G.	
CRICHTON, W.	LOGGIE, K.	**SEA SCOUTS**
CUNNINGHAM, B.	McDONALD, J.	BURROWS, F.
DAY, R.	MOIR, A.	DeRUYTER, P.
DODDS, C.J.	MOORMAN, O.H.	FERRIES, B.
DOWSE, C.	MORGAN, F.	MILLS, H.
DUGGAN, G.C.	MOSS, A.W.	NOBLE, J.
DUNCAN, D.J.W.	NARRAMORE, A.E.	ROBERTS, R.
DUNDON, S.	O'NEILL, J.	ROBERTS, W.F.
FITZPATRICK, G.J.	ORR, L.	SANKEY, E.
FOWLER, A.	QUIRK, P. ST.J.	TURNER, G.H.
GOODWIN, D.E.	REDMOND, R.D'C.	WALKER, T.
GOODWIN, M.A.	REYNOLDS, P.	WHELAN, G.

IN MEMORY OF THE
OFFICERS
NON COMMISSIONED OFFICERS
AND
TROOPERS
OF
THE SOUTH IRISH HORSE
WHO GAVE THEIR LIVES IN THE
1914.   GREAT WAR   1918.

And I saw Heaven opened, and behold a white horse: and
he that sat upon him was called Faithful and True, and
in righteousness he doth judge and make war.
And he was clothed with a vesture dipped in blood:
and his name is called The Word of God.
And the armies which were in heaven followed him upon
white horses, clothed in fine linen, white and clean.
And he hath on his vesture and on his thigh a name written,
KING OF KINGS, AND LORD OF LORDS.
(Rev. XIX)

ERECTED BY THEIR COMRADES.

*105–112. Typical Great War memorials. Clockwise
from far left.
105. St John's, Edgeworthstown, Co. Longford; 106.
Kilmore Cathedral, Co. Cavan; 107. St Patrick's
Cathedral; 108. Memorial in St Patrick's Cathedral;
109. St Mary's, Blessington, Co. Wicklow; 110. St
Patrick's, Monaghan; 111. St Multose's, Kinsale,
Co. Cork; 112. St Peter's, Bandon, Co. Cork.*

113. Great War memorial outside St Malachi's, Hillsborough, Co. Down.

pulpits can be seen at St Iberius's, Wexford, and Clonfeacle, Benburb, Co. Tyrone; impressive Celtic memorial crosses are sited at St Malachi's, Hillsborough, Co. Down, and St John the Baptist's, Clontarf, Co. Dublin.

Individual memorials, many of them beautifully designed, are to be found in most churches, the following being typical examples. Second Lieutenant John M. Vaughan (Dromore Cathedral, Co. Down) died of wounds, aged eighteen. Lieutenant Christopher B. Prior-Wandersforde (St Mary's, Castlecomer, Co. Kilkenny) died of wounds, aged twenty. Major William E. Parsons, 5th earl of Rosse (St Brendan's, Birr, Co. Offaly), died of wounds received three years earlier, aged 45. Lieutenant John F. C. Fogerty (St Columba's, Ennis, Co. Clare) was killed in action, aged 21.

Beside the memorial to the latter is the temporary wooden cross erected over his burial-place in Belgium and brought to Ireland when it was replaced by the simple standard headstone raised over the grave of every soldier, irrespective of rank. There is

114. St Nicholas's, Adare, Co. Limerick.

*115. St
Columba's, Ennis,
Co. Clare.*

*116. St Philip's and St James's,
Booterstown, Co. Dublin.*

IN LOVING MEMORY OF
EDMUND RICHARD FANE BECHER,
LIEUTENANT 8TH BATTS ROYAL MUNSTER FUSILIERS,
WHO DIED FROM WOUNDS, 19TH JULY 1916,
RECEIVED IN A BOMBING RAID AGAINST THE ENEMY'S
TRENCHES NEAR BETHUNE AND IS BURIED IN THE
COMMUNAL CEMETERY AT MAZINGARBE.
BORN 27TH MARCH 1897.

117. St Carthage's Cathedral, Lismore, Co. Waterford.

a similar cross in St Nicholas's Church, Adare, Co. Limerick, to Maurice Fitzgerald of the Irish Guards, who died of wounds in 1918, and in St Philip's and St James's, Booterstown, Co. Dublin, to Lieutenant John F. Healy, who was killed during the Battle of the Somme, aged nineteen. There is one in St Brigid's, Castleknock, Co. Dublin, to Lieutenant George Brooke, who died at the Battle of the Aisne in 1914. He is also remembered in the same church by a Harry Clarke stained glass window.

Captain Arthur Henry Eric Russell of the 6th Battalion,

118. The author's uncle, Samuel Victor Hutchison, killed on the Somme, aged 21. He has no known grave. (Photographer, R. Forbes, Dublin)

Connaught Rangers, was sixteen when he joined the army in 1914 and was mortally wounded four years later 'while gallantly leading his men in a counter attack' on the heights of St Emilie in France. His black and white marble memorial plaque with sword and regimental badges is in St Mary's, Moate, Co. Westmeath.

The loss suffered by some families must have been almost unbearable. A stained glass window by Lady Glenavy in Tullow Church, Foxrock, Co. Dublin, remembers the three sons of William Henry and Emily Charlotte Wilson who died in the war. A brass plaque in Waterford Cathedral reminds us that Colonel E. Roberts lost five grandsons, four in France and one at Gallipoli. Four grandsons of Peter Connellan were killed and are remembered in a beautiful stained glass window by Ethel Rhind in St Canice's Cathedral, Kilkenny. Six families in Monkstown, Dublin, each lost two sons.

Captain Standish George Smithwick, a regular soldier who had seen action in the Boer War and elsewhere, served with the 2nd Battalion, Royal Dublin Fusiliers, in France. During the famous

Christmas truce in 1914 he met and became friendly with a German officer. Some months later, when on a solo reconnaissance patrol, he suddenly found himself face to face with him again. Both stopped, said nothing, lowered their revolvers, turned their backs and moved away unharmed. This was prior to the battle in May 1915 at a place known as Mouse Trap Farm where the battalion suffered such huge losses that it barely survived as a unit. Captain Smithwick was badly wounded and twice gassed but survived the war. He died, aged 80, in 1958 and is buried with his second wife Marjorie in Monsea churchyard, near Dromineer, Co. Tipperary. Basil Maclear, a famous Irish rugby international, was among those killed at Mouse Trap Farm. Seven other Irish rugby internationals died in the war.

Twenty-five members of the Irish bar were among those who died. A fine stained glass window by Wilhelmina Geddes in St Ann's, Dawson Street, Dublin, remembers two killed at Suvla Bay, Gallipoli, in August 1915. They are Ernest Lawrence Julian (Royal Dublin Fusiliers) and Robert Hornidge Cullinan (Royal Munster Fusiliers), who were among the thousands of Irish dead and wounded in that murderous and failed campaign against the Turks.

119. Memorial to Ernest Lawrence Julian and Robert Hornidge Cullinan, killed at Suvla Bay, Gallipoli, in St Ann's, Dawson Street, Dublin (artist: Wilhelmina Geddes).

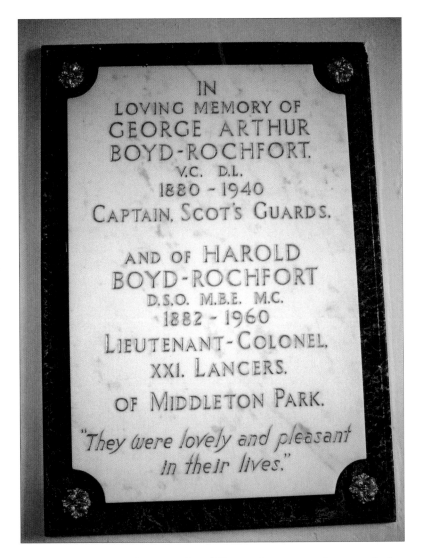

120. St Sinan's, Tyrellspass, Co. Westmeath.

Many memorials record soldiers who were decorated for bravery in actions that often involved hand-to-hand fighting. Conditions in the front-line trenches were appalling and, apart from the actual fighting, men lived in constant fear of shelling, plagued by lice and surrounded by rats feeding on unburied corpses. Thousands drowned in flooded shell holes or perished from the cold. For many it was hell on earth. Forty-five Irishmen won the Victoria Cross, many of whom have been forgotten and have no memorials. Some are still remembered in a tangible way, however.

Captain George Arthur Boyd-Rochfort VC (1880–1940) of the Scots Guards, then a second lieutenant, was supervising a working party in a front-line trench in France in August 1915 when a German mortar bomb landed on the parapet. He shouted a warning and rushed forward to hurl the bomb over the edge of the trench, where it exploded, thus saving the lives of many of his men. He was the first Guards' officer to win the Victoria Cross since the Crimean War, and when he returned to his native Westmeath he received a hero's welcome. Shortly afterwards he was decorated by King George V at Windsor Castle. Three of his cousins, all decorated soldiers, failed to survive the war. He shares his memorial in St Sinan's, Tyrellspass, Co. Westmeath, with his brother, Lieutenant Colonel Harold Boyd-Rochfort (1882–1960) of the 23rd Lancers.

An obelisk in the graveyard of Collon Church, Collon, Co. Louth, was raised in memory of Second Lieutenant James S. Emerson VC of the Royal Inniskilling Fusiliers, who showed heroic leadership during fierce fighting in France in 1917. During an attack, and as the only officer remaining in his company, he

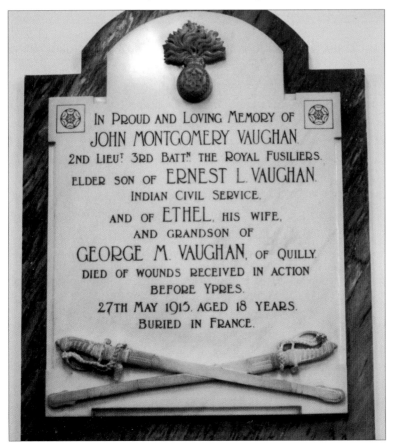

121. Dromore Cathedral, Co. Down.

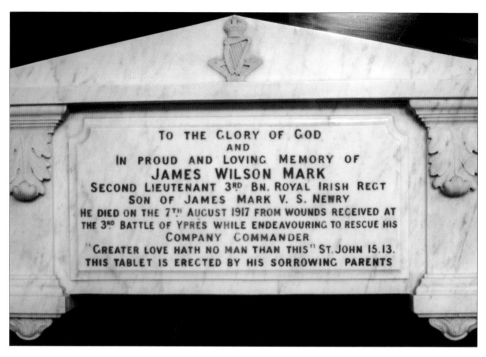

TO THE GLORY OF GOD
AND
IN PROUD AND LOVING MEMORY OF
JAMES WILSON MARK
SECOND LIEUTENANT 3ʳᵈ BN. ROYAL IRISH REGT
SON OF JAMES MARK V. S. NEWRY
HE DIED ON THE 7ᵀᴴ AUGUST 1917 FROM WOUNDS RECEIVED AT
THE 3ᴿᴰ BATTLE OF YPRES WHILE ENDEAVOURING TO RESCUE HIS
COMPANY COMMANDER
"GREATER LOVE HATH NO MAN THAN THIS" ST.JOHN 15.13.
THIS TABLET IS ERECTED BY HIS SORROWING PARENTS

122. St Mary's,
Newry, Co. Down.

cleared 400 yards of German trench, which he defended with a small force for over three hours despite being severely wounded. He then led his men in another assault, which allowed time for reinforcements to arrive, but died soon afterwards.

In June 1917, in France, Second Lieutenant John S. Dunville VC, whose memorial in the form of a Union flag is in Holywood Parish Church, Co. Down, was in charge of a party of sappers ordered to destroy the enemy's barbed wire. During the operation a problem arose, and Dunville placed himself between the corporal dealing with the difficulty and the Germans, as a result of which he was severely wounded. He nevertheless continued to direct his men until the operation was completed and walked unaided back to his lines, 'setting a magnificent example of courage, determination and devotion to duty'. He died the following day.

Also in France, in the same year, Corporal John Cunningham VC of the Leinster Regiment, a Lewis gunner, came under attack from twenty German storm troopers, whom he resisted until his ammunition ran out. He then left his position and engaged the enemy in the open with hand-grenades until these also were expended. Exhausted and badly wounded by bullets and shrapnel, he made his way back to his own lines, where he died four days later. His memorial tablet is in St Mary's, Thurles, Co. Tipperary.

123. To Henry Becher, killed in action March 1915, in Rosscarbery Cathedral, Co. Cork.

Wherefore take unto you the whole armour of GOD

To the Glory of GOD and in loving memory of
Henry Owen Dabridgecourt Becher
1st Cameronians killed in action at Bois Grenier
15 March 1915

Sergeant James Somers VC, Royal Inniskilling Fusiliers, found himself alone in a forward trench at Gallipoli in the Dardanelles in July 1915 when the men who were supposed to hold it withdrew. He held out for an entire night, and when reinforcements arrived in the morning he led an attack against the Turks and captured part of their trench. This position was held throughout the

124. *To Lieutenant Colonel John McDonnell, killed at Ypres in 1918, in St Mary's, Julianstown, Co. Louth.*

IN MEMORY OF
SERGEANT ROBERT QUIGG,
12TH BN. ROYAL IRISH RIFLES,
WHO WON THE
VICTORIA CROSS
FOR MOST CONSPICUOUS BRAVERY
AT THE BATTLE OF THE SOMME ON
IST JULY 1916.

BORN 12TH MARCH 1885,
DIED 14TH MAY 1955.
ERECTED BY HIS COMRADES.

125. Billy churchyard, Co. Antrim.

following day, during which he made frequent trips to the rear for water and ammunition. Later, in France, he was badly gassed and died soon after returning home in 1918. He is buried in St Kieran's churchyard, Cloughjordan, Co. Tipperary, where his father was sexton.

During the last great German offensive in France in 1918 Second Lieutenant Edmund de Wind VC, Royal Irish Rifles, held his front-line position near St Quentin almost single-handedly for seven hours despite being twice wounded. Later, with two other soldiers, he climbed up under machine-gun and rifle fire to clear the enemy out of a trench. He continued to repel attack after attack until fatally wounded. He is remembered by a marble tablet in St Mary's, Comber, Co. Down. A street in that town is also named after him.

Sergeant Robert Quigg VC, Royal Irish Rifles, survived the war

143

There was even greater loss of life when the passenger liner *Lusitania* was torpedoed off the Old Head of Kinsale in May 1915. In all, 1,198 people died, including Sir Hugh Lane (1875–1915), the art collector, who is remembered by a mural tablet in St Ann's, Dawson Street, Dublin. In the graveyard of St Multose's Church, Kinsale, Co. Cork, there are two small plots containing 'Victims of the *Lusitania* outrage'. This sinking was largely responsible for bringing the United States into the war.

The Great War ('the war to end all wars') ended at 11.00am on 11 November 1918, and the combatants returned home. Over 300,000 Irishmen had served in the British forces, and the beautiful Irish National War Memorial at Islandbridge on the banks of the River Liffey remembers the 49,400 who died. In many towns in Northern Ireland there are public memorials to the fallen but, with few exceptions, as at Bray, Co. Wicklow, no town in the Republic records their loss. When the Irish Free State came into existence in 1922 an era of revisionist history was introduced and those who participated in the war, whether Unionist or Nationalist, were intimidated or ignored and in time forgotten. The narrow nationalism practised in the south for most of the twentieth century even denied the survivors the right to remember their lost ones in public, and the wearing of a poppy on Remembrance Day was considered unpatriotic. Happily, there has been a change in public perception in recent years and especially since 1998, when President Mary McAleese and Queen Elizabeth jointly attended the opening of the Ireland for Peace Park on the site of the Battle of Messines, where in 1917 the Nationalist 16th Irish Division and the Unionist 36th Ulster Division fought side by side and captured one of the strongest German defensive positions on the western front.

12. THE SECOND WORLD WAR (1939–45)

I t is believed that 165,000 Irishmen and women, from every class and creed, joined the British forces during the Second World War. We know for certain that 4,543 died while serving in the army, but this may be a conservative figure as other sources put the total dead at between 14,000 and 15,000.

When war was declared in 1939 the Irish Free State had been independent for seventeen years, but most Protestants were still deeply attached to Britain and the British Empire. As a child the writer remembers services in St Thomas's Church, Mount Merrion, Co. Dublin, when prayers were said for the safety of our soldiers, sailors and airmen and their ultimate victory. Very often the congregation sang 'God save the King' before leaving. It is not surprising, therefore, that members of the Church of Ireland volunteered to serve in the war, many making the supreme sacrifice.

Their memorials, mainly individual, can be seen throughout the island. They reveal the world-wide nature of the conflict and the complexities of modern warfare. An early casualty was Second Lieutenant Ion Duncan Grove-White, who was killed, aged nineteen, on 21 May 1940 near Oudenarde as the British army retreated to Dunkirk. His memorial is in St Mary's, Doneraile, Co. Cork.

A year later Lieutenant Commander Hugh Tristram de la Poer Beresford RN was killed in action off the island of Crete. He was buried in Egypt on 27 June 1941 and his memorial tablet is in Holy Trinity, Clonegam, Co. Waterford. He was the third son of the 6th marquis of Waterford.

Pilot Officer John Samuel Victor Fegan RAF died in a bombing raid over Germany in July 1942, aged 24. He is remembered in Cavan Parish Church and the following is included in his epitaph:

To THE GLORY OF GOD
AND
IN PROUD AND HAPPY MEMORY OF
PILOT-OFFICER JOHN SAMUEL VICTOR FEGAN, RAFVR
OF THIS PARISH
AGED 24 YEARS
WHO WITH HIS GALLANT CREW FAILED TO RETURN
FROM OPERATIONS OVER GERMANY 19/20 JULY 1942

"O Valiant Hearts, Who to your Glory came
Through Dust of Conflict and through Battle-flame."

ERECTED BY HIS FAMILY

127. Cavan Parish Church.

'O Valiant Hearts, Who to your Glory came
Through Dust of Conflict and through Battle-flame'.

A beautiful memorial in St Mary's, Castlecomer, Co. Kilkenny, remembers Major Bryan Beresford-Gahan of the Royal Irish Fusiliers, who died of wounds in North Africa in January 1943, aged 26. He was buried in Tripoli Military Cemetery, Libya.

Major Astley John Cooper, a glider pilot with the First Airborne Division, was killed in July 1943 during the invasion of Sicily. He is buried at Catania British Cemetery on that island and is commemorated by a marble plaque in Cashel Cathedral, Co. Tipperary.

Major Richard Lawrence McKinley of the 16th Punjab Regiment, Indian army, was killed at the terrible Battle of Cassino in Italy on 16 March 1944, aged 25. His memorial is in St Mary's, Templemore, Co. Tipperary.

Captain Denis MacGillycuddy of the 47th Dragoon Guards was killed in Burma (now Myanmar) in 1944 while fighting with the 'Chindits' (a special long-range force) against the Japanese. He was 27 and his memorial is in Knockane Church, Co. Kerry (now deconsecrated).

128. St Mary's, Castlecomer, Co. Kilkenny.

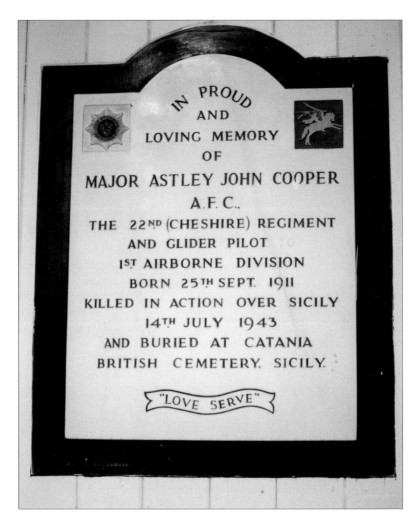

129. Cashel Cathedral, Co. Tipperary.

IN PROUD
AND
LOVING MEMORY
OF
MAJOR ASTLEY JOHN COOPER
A.F.C.,
THE 22ND (CHESHIRE) REGIMENT
AND GLIDER PILOT
1ST AIRBORNE DIVISION
BORN 25TH SEPT. 1911
KILLED IN ACTION OVER SICILY
14TH JULY 1943
AND BURIED AT CATANIA
BRITISH CEMETERY, SICILY.

"LOVE SERVE"

Although their aunt, Countess Markievicz, was an iconic figure in Republican Ireland, this did not prevent two of her nephews from serving and dying in the war. Sub-lieutenant Brian Gore-Booth RN drowned when his ship, HMS *Exmouth*, was sunk during convoy duty in 1940, while his brother, Lieutenant Hugh Gore-Booth of the Royal Irish Fusiliers, died in action on the island of Leros in the Aegean Sea in 1943. Their almost life-size portraits can be seen in a two-light memorial window by Catherine O'Brien in Lissadell Church, Co. Sligo.

Two other brothers are remembered by a marble plaque in Holy Trinity, Westport, Co. Mayo. They are Chief Petty Officer George F. Simmons, aged 29, and Petty Officer James F. B. Simmons, both of whom were killed in action aboard HMS *Gloucester* on 22 May 1941 during the German invasion of Crete.

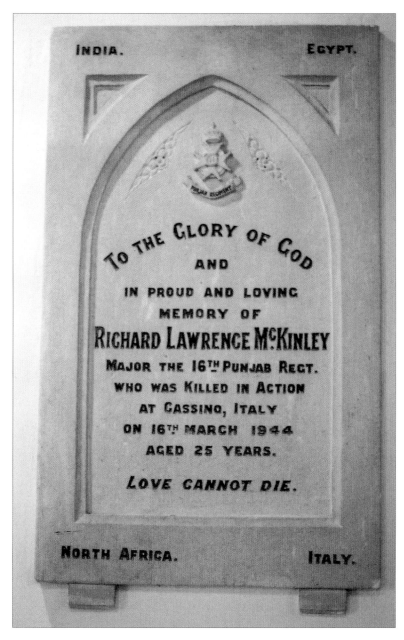

INDIA. EGYPT.

TO THE GLORY OF GOD
AND
IN PROUD AND LOVING
MEMORY OF
RICHARD LAWRENCE M^cKINLEY
MAJOR THE 16TH PUNJAB REGT.
WHO WAS KILLED IN ACTION
AT CASSINO, ITALY
ON 16TH MARCH 1944
AGED 25 YEARS.

LOVE CANNOT DIE.

NORTH AFRICA. ITALY.

130. St Mary's, Templemore, Co. Tipperary.

'Greater love hath no man than this,
that a man laid down his life for his friends.'

A wall-tablet in Christ Church, Delgany, Co. Wicklow, remembers
Patrick Oswald FitzGerald Hadoke, who died on 26 June 1944
while a prisoner of war of the Japanese. The latter ignored the
rights of prisoners as defined by the Geneva Convention of 1929,

151

*131. St Mary's,
Blessington, Co. Wicklow.*

132. St Mary's churchyard, Blessington, Co. Wicklow.

133 (top). Commonwealth graves, Eglantine churchyard, Co. Down.

134 (above). Commonwealth graves, Ballykelly, Co. Londonderry.

153

and thousands died as a result of malnutrition, slave labour and cruelties of every kind.

Other memorials remind us of those who met their end in Ireland. Four members of the Royal Air Force lie buried, side by side, in the graveyard of St Mary's, Blessington, Co. Wicklow. All were killed when their bomber, completely off course, crashed into Black Hill, Lacken, overlooking the Blessington Lakes, on 17 April 1941. Inside the church they are commemorated by an attractive plaque.

Many airmen flew from bases in Northern Ireland on bombing missions over Europe or attacking German warships and submarines in the Atlantic Ocean. Losses were heavy, and planes often returned with dead and wounded on board. Many of those who died were young men from Australia, Canada, New Zealand and South Africa, and they were laid to rest under military headstones in such places as Ballykelly, Co. Londonderry, Eglantine, Co. Down, and Limavady, Co. Londonderry. Their well-tended graves prove that their sacrifice, so far from home, has not been forgotten.

135. Christ Church graveyard, Limavady, Co. Londonderry.

Women played a very important role during the Second World War in the army, navy, airforce and nursing services. They were frequently exposed to enemy action and 52 from Ireland died, of whom 41 were from the Irish Free State. The name of one of the latter, Thelma Daphne Jackson, is included in the memorial to the seven parishioners of Monkstown who gave their lives in the cause of freedom.

13. THE TWENTIETH CENTURY

The nature, design and content of memorials in the first half of the twentieth century were little changed from the last decades of Queen Victoria's reign. There were, however, two notable differences: firstly, the numerous war memorials following the Boer War and the two World Wars, and, secondly, the very high standard of much of the stained glass. In the latter connection, An Tur Gloine (The Tower of Glass), founded in 1903 by Sarah Purser (1848–1943), produced work of outstanding quality and equal to the best in the world at that time. The artists working there included Michael Healy (1873–1941), Evie Hone (1894–1955), Alfred E. Child (1875–1939), Wilhelmina Geddes (1887–1955), Catherine O'Brien (1881–1963), Ethel Rhind (1879–1952), Beatrice Elvery (1889–1931) and Hubert McGoldrick (1897–1967), who between them produced over 300 memorial windows in 162 Church of Ireland churches. Harry Clarke (1889–1931), who worked outside the Tur Gloine circle, is the greatest Irish stained glass artist and has windows in nine churches. One of his finest is in memory of Percy La Touche and his wife Annette in St Patrick's, Carnalway, Co. Kildare. The former was the last of his line to live in the adjoining Harristown estate and was the brother of Rose Lucy La Touche (1848–75), who romantically attached to the famous writer, artist and critic John Ruskin (1819–1900). He first met her when she was ten, and for the next seventeen years was totally obsessed with 'the wild rose of Kildare'. She loved him too, but for religious and other reasons her parents would not agree to their marriage. When Rose fell ill and died at the age of 27 Ruskin was overcome with grief from which he never fully recovered.

There are two interesting memorials at Drumcondra, Dublin. Firstly, a metal plaque on the wall just inside the entrance to the graveyard, where he is buried, remembers Patrick Heeney (1882–1911), who composed the music of 'The Soldier's Song', the Irish national anthem. His friend Peadar Kearney (1883–1942)

136. Lady Enid Layard (d. 1912) in St Paul's, Piltown, Co. Kilkenny.

137. *In memory of Catherine Traill (d. 1909) in Billy Church, Co. Antrim (artist: Michael Healy).*

138 (above). Christ Church, Gorey, Co. Wexford (artist: Harry Clarke).

139 (right). Memorial to her sisters, Henrietta, Norah and Beatrice, by the artist Catherine O'Brien in St Columba's, Ennis, Co. Clare.

wrote the words. Secondly, there is the grave of Seamus McGowan (1874–1963), who is said to have been the model for the IRA man Maguire in Seán O'Casey's play *The shadow of a gunman*. The granite headstone refers to his membership of the Irish Citizen Army and is engraved with the plough and the stars.

The second half of the century brought radical change to every aspect of Irish life. Old certainties were undermined and society became much more secular, as the following selection of epitaphs on tombstones erected in the Republic between 1973 and 2001 clearly confirms:

140. In memory of the
6th earl of Courtown (d.
1933) in Kiltennel
Church, Co. Wexford
(artist: Hubert
McGoldrick).

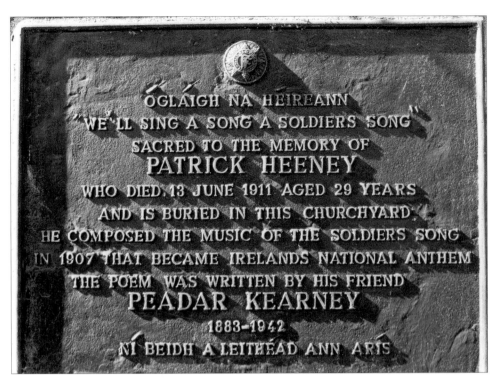

ÓGLÁIGH NA hÉIREANN
"WE'LL SING A SONG A SOLDIERS SONG"
SACRED TO THE MEMORY OF
PATRICK HEENEY
WHO DIED 13 JUNE 1911 AGED 29 YEARS
AND IS BURIED IN THIS CHURCHYARD
HE COMPOSED THE MUSIC OF THE SOLDIERS SONG
IN 1907 THAT BECAME IRELANDS NATIONAL ANTHEM
THE POEM WAS WRITTEN BY HIS FRIEND
PEADAR KEARNEY
1883-1942
NÍ BEIDH A LEITHÉAD ANN ARÍS

*141. Drumcondra graveyard,
Dublin.*

*142. St Mary's graveyard,
Rathvilly, Co. Carlow.*

SCUTO AMORIS DIVINI

JOHN
JACKSON
A GEOLOGIST.
1920 - 1992.
21-2-20 — 19-11-91.

MICHAEL CRICHTON
1909 - 1990

COMMANDER, R.N.
COMMISSIONER FOR SCOUTS Co. FERMANAGH
ADMIRAL, L.F.Y.C.

ANNA

143 (left). Teampall na mBocht, Toormore, Co. Cork.

144 (right). Holy Trinity churchyard, Crom, Co. Fermanagh.

145. St James's churchyard, Durrus, Co. Cork.

'The inventing farmer—sorely missed'
(Derrylossary, Co. Wicklow)

'Set the stars ablaze'
(Trim Cathedral, Co. Meath)

'A wonderful life'
(St Multose's, Kinsale, Co. Cork)

'And one by one they crept silently to rest'
(Kilbixy, Co. Westmeath)

'And the cow jumped over the moon'
(St Mary's, Dungarvan, Co. Waterford)

'Here lies poor but honest
Cecil Pratt
He was
a most excellent angler
until
death envious of his merit
threw out his line, hooked him
and landed him here 14 June 1973 aged 67 years'
(St Mary's, Youghal, Co. Cork)

Good-humoured epitaphs are not common in Northern Ireland, where 3,200 people died during three decades of futile and bitter civil war. Three hundred members of the Royal Ulster Constabulary were killed in the line of duty and, in all, the security forces lost 950 men and women. The tablets on the walls of many churches bear witness to their sacrifice and to the many civilians who also died.

Relatively few traditional memorials are to be seen from the second half of the century, but one worthy of mention and beautifully carved is that to Laurence Michael Harvey Parsons, 6th earl of Rosse (1906–79), and his wife Anne (1902–92) in St Brendan's, Birr, Co. Offaly. There is also the fine tomb of the earls and countesses of Wicklow in the graveyard at St Brigid's, Kilbride, Co. Wicklow, which includes the body of the 8th and last earl, William Cecil James Howard (1902–78). Less traditional but still very fine is the entrance door to Newcastle Church, Co. Wicklow,

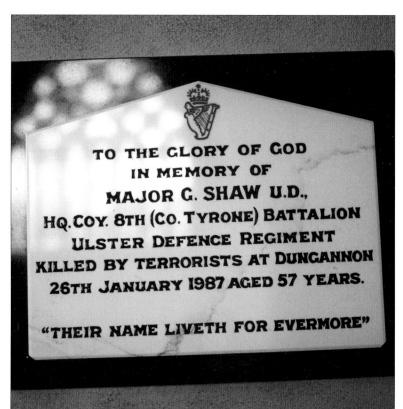

TO THE GLORY OF GOD
IN MEMORY OF
MAJOR G. SHAW U.D.,
HQ.COY. 8TH (Co. TYRONE) BATTALION
ULSTER DEFENCE REGIMENT
KILLED BY TERRORISTS AT DUNGANNON
26TH JANUARY 1987 AGED 57 YEARS.

"THEIR NAME LIVETH FOR EVERMORE"

146. St Anne's, Dungannon, Co. Tyrone.

147. Royal Ulster Constabulary memorial in Clonfeakle Parish Church, Benburb, Co. Tyrone.

163

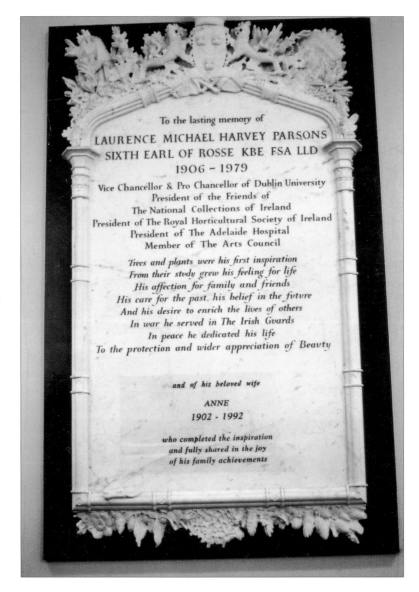

*148. St
Brendan's, Birr,
Co. Offaly.*

in memory of Augustus Kennedy Kisch, who died in 1977 (sculptor: Imogen Stuart). Also of interest is the memorial in St Peter's, Bandon, Co. Cork, to the last earl of Bandon, Percy Ronald Gardner Bernard, who was air chief marshal of the Royal Air Force and died in 1979.

The Cathedral Church of St Anne in Belfast must be one of the very few cathedrals to have only one person buried within its walls. This is Sir Edward Carson (1854–1935), whose tomb is situated halfway down the south aisle. Sir Edward was leader of the Ulster Unionist Party during the Home Rule crisis of 1911/1922, and is

149. Memorial to the countess of Wicklow in St Brigid's graveyard, Kilbride, Co. Wicklow.

also famous as the defence lawyer for the marquess of Queensbury at the 'first trial' of Oscar Wilde in 1895. The memorial plaque was designed by Rosamund Praeger.

After the Second World War southern Irishmen continued to serve in the British army, and Lieutenant Charles Godfrey Alexander of the King's Royal Irish Hussars was killed in action during the Korean War (1950–3), aged 23. This conflict between communist and non-communist countries ended in the partition of Korea. Britain was one of many countries that fought in a United Nations army and, in addition to the Hussars, two other Irish regiments—the Royal Ulster Rifles and the Inniskilling Fusiliers—

150. Door of Newcastle Church, Co. Wicklow, in memory of Augustus Kennedy Kisch, who died in 1977.

were involved. All three suffered heavy casualties, mainly at the hands of the Chinese. There is a memorial to Lieutenant Alexander in St Carthage's Cathedral, Lismore, Co. Waterford.

During this century two presidents of the Republic were members of the Church of Ireland. Dr Douglas Hyde (1860–1949), scholar, linguist and co-founder of the Gaelic League, became the first president, serving from 1938 to 1945. He is remembered by a bust in St Patrick's Cathedral and is buried under a Celtic cross in the graveyard at Tibohine Church, near Frenchpark, Co. Roscommon, where his father was rector. Erskine Hamilton Childers (1905–74) was born in London but worked with the *Irish Press* newspaper until he became a Fianna Fáil TD in 1938. After a long political career, during which he held many government posts, he was elected president in 1973 but died suddenly the

151. Tibohine churchyard, Frenchpark, Co. Roscommon.

152. Grave of President Erskine Childers at Derrylossary churchyard, Co. Wicklow.

153. Seat at St Patrick's, Kenmare, Co. Kerry, in memory of Robert and Lily Topham.

following year. He is buried under a granite cross in the graveyard of the deconsecrated and roofless Derrylossary Church, near Roundwood, Co. Wicklow. His epitaph includes the prayer:

154. Ancient and modern at St Brigid's, Stillorgan, Co. Dublin.

'God be in my head and in my understanding,
God be in my eyes and in my looking,
God be in my mouth and in my speaking,
God be in my heart and in my thinking,
God be at mine end and at my departing'.

Attitudes to death have varied over the centuries, and one of the most significant changes in Ireland in the twentieth century has been the acceptance of cremation. Up to the nineteenth century it had been forbidden by the western Christian Church, but because of urban overcrowding gradually became acceptable. It does not, however, encourage great memorials and, instead, most churchyards now have a 'Garden of Remembrance', where small tablets remembering those cremated line the walls or are embedded in the ground. Otherwise, many modern memorials are of a practical nature and frequently involve the presentation to a church of such items as prayer-desks and communion plate. Seats in the grounds are also popular, as is the planting of trees. It can be said with certainty that the great days of monuments and mausoleums are dead and gone. We should cherish those that survive.

14. LIST OF SCULPTORS

John Bacon the Elder (1740–99)
A prolific English sculptor responsible for two Irish memorials.

John Bacon the Younger (1777–1859)
Son of John Bacon the Elder and creator of a number of Irish monuments.

Sir Joseph Edgar Boehm RA (1834–90)
Born in Austria, he settled in England, where he had a highly successful career and was sculptor-in-ordinary to Queen Victoria.

Albert Bruce-Joy (1842–1924)
A Belfast sculptor and student of John Henry Foley.

Thomas Campbell (1790–1858)
A Scottish sculptor who had studios in London and Rome.

Sir Francis Chantrey RA (1781–1841)
One of the finest English sculptors, famous for his public statues and church memorials. Three of the latter are in Ireland.

Sir Henry Cheere (1703–81)
A distinguished English sculptor. His monuments to Lord Doneraile and the earl of Kildare are his only known Irish work.

Patrick Cunningham (died 1774)
A Dublin-born artist best known as a wax-modeller.

Terence Farrell RHA (1798–1876)
Born in County Longford, he specialised in miniature busts. His other work includes one of the rectangular bronze reliefs on the Wellington monument in the Phoenix Park, Dublin.

Sir Thomas Farrell RHA (1827–1900)

Born in Dublin and son of Terence Farrell, he had a successful practice in the late nineteenth century in portrait and commemorative work. His best-known work is probably the statue of Lord Ardilaun in St Stephen's Green, Dublin.

John Flaxman RA (1755–1826)

Celebrated English sculptor and book illustrator. His best-known monuments are those of Lord Mansfield in Westminster Abbey and Lord Nelson in St Paul's Cathedral.

John Henry Foley RA, RHA (1818–74)

Born in Dublin, he was one of the outstanding sculptors of his day. Although his studio was in England, he produced many Dublin public statues, including those of Burke, Goldsmith, Grattan and O'Connell. His best-known English work is the Prince Consort and the group 'Asia' on the Albert Memorial in London.

J. Forsyth

A nineteenth-century English sculptor.

T. H. Hartley

A late nineteenth-century London sculptor.

James Heffernan (1785–1847)

Born in Cork, he worked all his life in the studio of Sir Francis Chantrey in England. Late in his life he returned to Ireland, where he died of dysentery.

John Hickey (1756–95)

Born in Dublin, he moved in 1777 to England, where he was sculptor to the prince of Wales. He was a very talented artist who died, aged 39, at the height of his career. According to a contemporary, 'intemperance abolished his powers and eclipsed his glory'.

Alexander Hills

A seventeenth-century sculptor with a studio in Holborn, London.

John Hogan (1800–58)
Born in Cork, he lived in Rome for 25 years and returned to Ireland in 1848. He was the most classical of all nineteenth-century Irish sculptors and specialised in religious subjects.

John Valentine Hogan (died 1920)
The son of his more famous sculptor father, John Hogan, he has statues in the pro-cathedral, Dublin.

William Kidwell (1662–1736)
A talented sculptor, born in Surrey, England, who spent the last 25 years of his life in Ireland, where his work, mainly for churches, was highly prized.

Patrick Kerin
An early seventeenth-century sculptor working in Kilkenny, Limerick and Tipperary.

Thomas Kirk RHA (1781–1845)
Born in Cork, he was a leading Irish sculptor in the first half of the nineteenth century. His best-known work was the statue of Admiral Nelson on his pillar in Dublin, destroyed by the IRA in 1966.

Joseph Robinson Kirk RHA (1821–94)
Son of Thomas Kirk and a prolific sculptor. He is responsible for one of the bronze reliefs on the Wellington monument, Dublin.

Lewis of Cheltenham
An early nineteenth-century family firm of sculptors responsible for several Irish monuments.

Samuel Ferres Lynn RHA (1834–76)
Born in County Tipperary, he worked mainly in Belfast and London, specialising in public statues. He was one of four Irish sculptors employed on the Albert Memorial.

Patrick McDowell RA (1790–1870)
Born in Belfast, he spent most of his life in England, where his best-known work is 'Europe' on the Albert Memorial. Along with John Henry Foley, he was the most important Irish sculptor of

the nineteenth century.

Samuel Manning the Elder (1788–1842)
A pupil and later partner of John Bacon the Elder.

Christopher Moore (1790–1863)
Born in Dublin, he specialised in portrait busts. He spent the last 40 years of his life in London and was a regular exhibitor at the Royal Academy.

Sir Richard Morrison (1767–1849)
Born in County Cork, he was an architect who occasionally designed memorials.

Joseph Nollekens RA (1737–1823)
A fashionable and highly successful English portrait sculptor.

Rosamond (Sophia) Praeger (1867–1954)
A sculptor and illustrator born in Holywood, Co. Down.

Charles Regnart of London (1759–1844)

Edward Richardson (1812–69)
A London sculptor who specialised in the restoration of medieval statues and monuments.

J. Robinson and Son
 A late nineteenth-century Belfast firm.

John Michael Rysbrack (1694–1770)
Born in Antwerp, he was a leading sculptor in England in the early eighteenth century.

Peter Scheemakers (1691–1781)
Born in Antwerp, he spent most of his life in England. He established his reputation with a statue of Shakespeare for Westminster Abbey.

David Sheehan (died 1756)
A leading Dublin stonemason and sculptor employed on major building projects in the city.

Edward Smyth (1745–1812)
Born in County Meath, he is famous as the sculptor of much of the decorative carving on the Custom House, the Four Courts and King's Inns, Dublin.

John Smyth ARHA (*c.* 1773–1840)
Son of Edward Smyth, he was responsible for many statues on Dublin public buildings, including the General Post Office and the College of Surgeons.

William Spence (1793–1849)
A Liverpool sculptor responsible for at least six Irish memorials.

Imogen Stuart (1927–)
Born in Berlin, she came to Ireland in 1949. An artist in stone, metal, clay, wood and stained glass, her work can be seen in many churches and public places throughout Ireland.

Edward (or Edmund) Tingham
An early seventeenth-century sculptor who also worked as an architect and builder.

John Van Nost the Younger (*c.* 1712–80)
Born in London, he settled about 1749 in Dublin, where he had a very successful practice. His church memorials are large-scale and impressive.

Sir Richard Westmacott RA (1775–1856)
A well-known English sculptor and chimney-piece designer who studied under Canova in Rome.

BIBLIOGRAPHY

Adams, D. 2003 An Irishman's Diary. *The Irish Times*, 7 June 2003.

Arthur, M. 2004 *Symbol of courage*. London.

Bateson, R. 2004 *The end—graves of Irish writers*. Kilcock.

Bowe, N.G., Caron, D. and Wynne, M. 1988 *Gazetteer of Irish stained glass*. Exeter.

Bryant, A. 1954 *The age of elegance*. Edinburgh.

Burke, T. 2005 *The 2nd Battalion, Royal Dublin Fusiliers*. Dublin.

Butler, M. 1972 *Maria Edgeworth*. Oxford.

Caldicott, C.E.J., Gough, H. and Pittion, J.P. 1987 *The Huguenots and Ireland*. Dublin.

Casey, C. and Rowan, A. 1993 *The buildings of north Leinster*. London.

Chambers, A. 2004 *At arm's length*. Dublin.

Churchill, W.S. 1930 *My early life*. London.

Comerford, P. 2005 An Irishman's Diary. *The Irish Times*, 2 April 2005.

Corlett, C. 1999 *Antiquities of Rathdown*. Bray.

Craig, M. 1997 *The architecture of Ireland to 1880*. Portrane.

Craig, M. 1999 *Mausolea Hibernica*. Dublin.

Doherty, R. and Truesdale, D. 2000 *Irish winners of the Victoria Cross*. Dublin.

Dunlop, R. 1982 *Plantation of renown*. Naas.

Foster, R.F. 1989 *The Oxford illustrated history of Ireland*. New York.

Graham, Rev. M. 2002 *St Peter's, Drogheda*. Drogheda.

Harbison, P., Potterton, H. and Sheehy, J. 1978 *Irish art and architecture*. London.

Hibbert, C. 1978 *The great mutiny*. London.

Howley, J. 1993 *The follies and garden buildings of Ireland*. London.

Igoe, V. 2001 *Dublin burial grounds and graveyards*. Dublin.

Ingram, J.A. 1997 *The cure of souls*. Dublin.

Jackson, V. 1987 *The monuments in St Patrick's Cathedral, Dublin*. Dublin.

Kerr, P. 2000 *The Crimean War*. London.

Kinsella, S. 2004 *Visitor's guide to Christ Church Cathedral, Dublin*. Dublin.

Lalor, B. (ed.) 2003 *The encyclopaedia of Ireland*. Dublin.

MacCarthy, R. 1995 *Ancient and modern*. Dublin.

Maye, B. 2005 An Irishman's Diary. *The Irish Times*, 4 April 2005.

Milne, K. [no date] *A history of the Church of Ireland*. Belfast.

Moffatt, M. 2004 An Irishman's Diary. *The Irish Times*, 17 January 2004.

Muir, D. 1996 *A brief guide to Christ Church, Delgany*.

Mulvihill, M. 2002 *Ingenious Ireland*. Dublin.

Mulvihill, M. 2005 An Irishwoman's Diary. *The Irish Times*, 5 May 2005.

Murphy, E. 2003 *A glorious extravaganza*. Bray.

Murray, B. 2002 *Epitaph of 1798*. Enniscorthy.

Myers, K. 2004 An Irishman's Diary. *The Irish Times*, 12 November 2004.

O'Brien, J. with Guinness, D. 1994 *Dublin—a grand tour*. London.

Pakenham, T. 1979 *The Boer War*. London.

Potterton, H. 1974 *Irish church monuments 1570–1880*. Belfast.

Power, D. and Sleeman, M. 1992 The Church of Ireland, Doneraile. *Mallow Field Club Journal* No. 10.

Rowan, A. 1979 *The buildings of Ireland—north west Ulster*. London.

Ruddock, Rev. N. and Kloss, N. 1997 *Unending worship*. Wexford.

Shuckburgh, E.S. 1902 *Two biographies of William Bedell*. Cambridge.

Walker, S. 2000 *Historic Ulster churches*. Belfast.

Whiteside, L. 1990 *George Otto Simms*. Trowbridge.

Williams, J. 1994 *Architecture in Ireland 1837–1921*. Dublin.

THE FOLLOWING ALSO PROVIDED USEFUL INFORMATION:

A short guide to St Anne's Cathedral, Belfast [no date].

A short guide to St Columb's Cathedral, Londonderry [no date].

A short guide to St Mary's Church, Newry [no date].

A short illustrated guide to the Parish of Holywood, Co. Down (2000).

Archaeology Ireland (Winter 2003).

Ardamine and Killena parishes (1987).

Celebrating 400 years (1596–1996)—a history of All Saints Parish Church, Antrim (1996).

Christ Church Cathedral, Lisburn—a brief illustrated guide (1993).

Country Life, 13 July 1978.

Country Life, 9 September 1982.

Hillsborough Parish Church—an illustrated visitor's guide (2000).

History of St Michael's Church, Castle Caulfield (1985).

Holy Trinity, Westport—a guide for visitors (1998).

'Inspiring stones'—a history of the dioceses of Limerick, Aghadoe, Killaloe, Kilfenora, Clonfert, Kilmacduagh and Emly (1995).

Kilternan Church 1826–1976 (Dublin, 1976).

Rosscarbery Cathedral—visitor's guide (1999).

St Audoen's, Dublin—a visitor's guide (2000).

St Barrahane's Church, Castletownsend [no date].

St Mary's Cathedral, Limerick (1999).

St Multose, Kinsale—a visitor's guide (1992).

St Patrick's, Monaghan (2002).

St Peter's, Bandon—an illustrated guide (1999).

Taney Parish News Magazine, February and December 2004.

The autobiography of Archibald Hamilton Rowan (Irish University Press, 1972).

The C. S. Lewis Centenary Trail (Belfast, 1998).

The Church of Ireland in County Meath (Trim, 1993).

The history of Lisburn Cathedral (Lisburn, 1993).

Visitor's guide to Armagh Cathedral (2001).

Visitors' guide to Dromore Cathedral [no date].

Visitor's guide to Kilmore Cathedral [no date].

Visitor's guide to St Ann's Church, Dublin (1999).

Visitor's guide to St Audoen's Church, Dublin [no date].

Visitor's guide to St Canice's Cathedral, Kilkenny (2000).

Visitor's guide to Sligo Cathedral [no date].

Visitor's guide to Waterford Cathedral [no date].

INDEX